Miss (Jane) Bowdler

Poems and Essays

Miss (Jane) Bowdler

Poems and Essays

ISBN/EAN: 9783337005382

Printed in Europe, USA, Canada, Australia, Japan

Cover: Foto ©Thomas Meinert / pixelio.de

More available books at **www.hansebooks.com**

POEMS AND ESSAYS,

BY THE LATE

MISS BOWDLER.

———

THE SEVENTH EDITION.

PUBLISHED FOR

THE BENEFIT OF THE GENERAL HOSPITAL AT BATH.

———

Vattene in pace alma beata et bella!
Vattene in pace a la fuperna fede,
E lafcia al mondo efempio di tua fede!

ARIOSTO.

BATH, PRINTED BY R. CRUTTWELL;

AND SOLD BY

DILLY, POULTRY, J. ROBSON AND T. HOOKHAM, NEW BOND-
STREET, LONDON; AND N. R. CHEYNE, EDINBURGH.

———

M DCC XCIII.

PREFACE.

THE following Poems and Eſſays were written to relieve the tedious hours of pain and ſickneſs. The Reader who ſeeks for amuſement only, may poſſibly receive no gratification from the peruſal of them; but for ſuch readers they are not intended.

To the humble and pious Chriſtian, who feels the preſſure of diſtreſs, and ſeeks in Religion for that ſupport and conſolation which nothing elſe can beſtow; to him is preſented an example of patience and reſignation which no ſufferings could conquer.

He will not find in the following pages the pride of Stoiciſm, or the cold precepts of unfeeling proſperity. The Author of theſe Eſſays felt,

felt, with the keeneſt ſenſibility, the uncommon misfortune which condemned her for ten years, in the prime of life, to conſtantly increaſing ſufferings; but ſhe found, in the principles which are here laid down, ſuch motives of conſolation as rendered her ſuperior to all the ſorrows of life, and to the lingering tortures of a moſt painful death.

They who were preſent at that awful ſcene, can need no other evidence in ſupport of a truth which the reader will find often repeated in theſe Eſſays, viz. that " though Religion " cannot prevent loſſes and diſappointments, " pains and ſorrows; yet in the midſt of them " all, and when every earthly pleaſure fails, it " commands, it inſtructs, it enables us to be " happy."

CONTENTS.

POEMS.

ESSAYS.

POEMS.

ODE

TO

HOPE.

I.

FRIEND to the wretch whofe bofom knows no joy!
  Parent of blifs beyond the reach of fate!
    Celeftial HOPE! thou gift divine,
    Sweet balm of grief! oh, ftill be mine.
  When pains torment, and cares annoy,
  Thou only canft their force abate,
And gild the gloom which fhades this mortal ftate.
    Though oft thy joys are falfe and vain,
    Though anxious doubts attend thy train,
    Though difappointment mock thy care,
    And point the way to fell defpair,
  Yet ftill my fecret foul fhall own thy pow'r
In forrow's bittereft pang, in pleafure's gayeft hour.

B

For from the date of Reafon's birth
　　That wond'rous pow'r was given,
　To foften every grief on earth,
　　'To raife the foul from thoughtlefs mirth,
　　　And wing its flight to heaven.
Nor pain nor pleafure can its force deftroy,
In every varied fcene it points to future joy.

II.

Fancy, wave thy airy pinions,
　　Bid the foft ideas rife,
　Spread o'er all thy wide dominions
　　Vernal fweets and cloudlefs fkies.
And lo! on yonder verdant plain,
　A lovely Youthful Train appear,
Their gentle hearts have felt no pain,
　Their guiltlefs bofoms know no fear:
In each gay fcene fome new delight they find,
Yet fancy gayer profpects ftill behind.
　　Where are the foft delufions fled?
　　Muft wifdom teach the foul to mourn?
Return, ye days of ignorance, return:
Before my eyes your fairy vifions fpread!
　Alas! thofe vifions charm no more,
　　The pleafing dream of youth is o'er;
Far other thoughts muft now the foul employ,
It glows with other hopes, it pants for other joy.

III.

The trumpet founds to War:
Loud fhouts re-echo from the mountain's fide,
The din of battle thunders from afar,
The foaming torrent rolls a crimfon tide;
The Youthful Warrior's breaft with ardour glows,
In thought he triumphs o'er ten thoufand foes:
Elate with hope he rufhes on,
The battle feems already won,
The vanquifh'd hofts before him fly,
His heart exults in fancied victory,
Nor heeds the flying fhaft, nor thinks of danger nigh.
Methinks I fee him now—
Fall'n his creft—his glory gone—
The opening laurel faded on his brow—
Silent the trump of his afpiring fame!
No future age fhall hear his name,
But darknefs fpread around her fable gloom,
And deep oblivion reft upon his tomb.

IV.

Through feas unknown, to diftant lands,
In queft of gain the bold Advent'rer goes,
Fearlefs roves o'er Afric's fands,
India's heats, or Zembla's fnows:
Each rifing day his dang'rous toil renews;
But toils and dangers check his courfe in vain:
Cheer'd by Hope, he ftill purfues

Fancy'd good through real pain,
Still in thought enjoys the prize,
And future happy days in long fucceffion rife:
Yet all his blifs a moment may deftroy,
Frail are his brighteft hopes, uncertain all his joy.

V.

Hark! the fprightly voice of Pleafure
  Calls to yonder rofy bower,
There fhe fcatters all her treafure,
  There exerts her magic power.
Liften to the pleafing call,
Follow, Mortals, follow all;
Lead the dance, and fpread the feaft,
Crown with rofes every gueft:
Now the fprightly minftrels found,
Pleafure's voice is heard around,
And Pleafure's fprightly voice the hills and dales
  refound.
Whence rofe that fecret figh?—
What fudden gloom o'erclouds thy cheerful brow?
Say, does not every pleafure wait thee now,
That e'er could charm the ear, or court the eye?—
  In vain does Nature lavifh all her ftore;
    The confcious fpirit ftill afpires,
    Still purfues fome new defires,
And every wifh obtain'd, it fighs and pants for more.

VI.

Are thefe, O Hope! the glories of thy reign?
 The airy dreams of Fancy and of Youth!
Muft all thy boafted pleafures lead to pain;
 Thy joys all vanifh at the light of truth?
Muft wretched man, led by a meteor fire,
  To diftant bleffings ftill afpire;
  Still with ardour ftrive to gain
  Joys he oft purfues in vain,
  Joys which quickly muft expire;
And when at length the fatal hour is come,
And death prepares th' irrevocable doom,
Mourn all his darling hopes at once deftroy'd,
And figh to leave that blifs he ne'er enjoy'd?

VII.

 Rife, Heavenly Vifions! rife,
And every vain delufive fear controul;
Let real glory charm my wond'ring eyes,
 And real happinefs enchant my foul!—
Hail glorious dawn of everlafting day!
 Though faintly feen at diftance here,
 Thy beams the finking heart can cheer,
And light the weary pilgrim on his way:
 For not in vain did Heaven infpire
 That active fpark of facred fire,
Which ftill with reftlefs ardour glows:
In pain, in pleafure, ftill the fame,

It feeks that heaven from whence it came,
And fcorns all meaner joys, all tranfient woes.
The foul, for perfect blifs defign'd,
Strives in vain that blifs to find,
'Till, wing'd by HOPE, at length it flies
Beyond the narrow bounds of earth, and air, and fkies.

VIII.

Still unmov'd, let HOPE remain
Fix'd on true fubftantial joy;
Dangers then fhall threat in vain,
Pains torment, or cares annoy:
Then fhall ev'ry guiltlefs pleafure
Smile with charms unknown before,
HOPE, fecure in real treafure,-
Mourn her blafted joys no more:
Then through each revolving year—
Though earthly glories fade away,
Though youth, and ftrength, and life itfelf, decay—
Yet ftill more bright the profpect fhall appear;
Happier ftill the lateft day, ·
Brighteft far the parting ray.
O'er life's laft fcene celeftial beams fhall fhine,
'Till death at length fhall burft the chain,
While fongs of triumph found on high;
Then fhall HOPE her power refign,
Loft in endlefs extacy,
And never-fading joy in Heaven's full glories reign.

ON THE

DEATH

OF

Mr. GARRICK.

THE laſt ſad rites were done—the ſacred ground
  Was clos'd—and GARRICK's duſt to duſt return'd;
In life, in death, with general honours crown'd,
  A nation own'd his worth—applauded—mourn'd.

For who, like him, could every ſenſe controul,
  To *Shakeſpeare*'s ſelf new charms, new force, impart;
Bid unknown horrors ſhake the firmeſt ſoul,
  And unknown feelings melt the hardeſt heart?

Oft when his eye, with more than magic pow'r,
  Gave life to thoughts which words could ne'er reveal,
The voice of praiſe awhile was heard no more,
  All gaz'd in ſilence, and could only feel.

Each thought ſuſpended in a general pauſe,
  All ſhar'd his paſſions, and forgot their own—
'Till rous'd at length, in thunders of applauſe,
  Th' accordant dictates of each heart were known.

O loft for ever to our wond'ring view!—
    Yet faithful memory fhall preferve thy name;
E'en diftant times thy honours fhall renew,
    And *Garrick* ftill fhall fhare his *Shakefpeare*'s fame.

Thus mufing, through the lonely aile I ftray'd,
    Recall'd the wonders of his matchlefs pow'rs,
And many a former fcene in thought furvey'd,
    While all unheeded pafs'd the filent hours.

With mournful awe I trod the facred ftones,
    Where kings and heroes fleep in long repofe,
And trophies, mould'ring o'er the warrior's bones,
    Proclaim how frail the life which fame beftows.

Now funk the laft faint beam of clofing day,
    Each form was loft, and hufh'd was ev'ry found;
All, all was filent as the fleeping clay,
    And darknefs fpread her fable veil around.

At once, methought, a more than midnight gloom
    With deathlike horror chill'd my throbbing breaft,
When lo! a voice, deep murmuring from the tomb,
    Thefe awful accents on my foul impreft:—

" Vain are the glories of a nation's praife;
    " The boaft of wit, the pride of genius, vain:
" A long, long night fucceeds the tranfient blaze,
    " Where darknefs, folitude, and filence, reign.

" The fhouts of loud applaufe which thoufands gave,
 " On me nor pride, nor pleafure, now beftow:
" Like the chill blaft that murmurs o'er my grave,
 " They pafs away—nor reach the duft below.

" One virtuous deed, to all the world unknown,
 " Outweighs the higheft blifs which thefe can give,
" Can cheer the foul when youth and ftrength are flown,
 " In ficknefs triumph, and in death furvive.

" What though to thee, in life's remoteft fphere,
 " Nor nature's gifts, nor fortune's, are confign'd,
" Let brighteft profpects to thy foul appear,
 " And hopes immortal elevate thy mind.

" The fculptur'd marble fhall diffolve in duft,
 " And fame, and wealth, and honours, pafs away:
" Not fuch the triumphs of the good and juft,
 Not fuch the glories of eternal day.

" Thefe, thefe fhall live, when ages are no more,
 " With never-fading luftre ftill fhall fhine:——
" Go then, to Heaven devote thy utmoft pow'r,
 " And know—whoe'er thou art—the prize is thine."

A

BALLAD.*

"RETURN, return, my haplefs fpoufe,
  " Nor feek the fatal place,
" Where thoughtlefs crowds expecting ftand
  " To fee thy child's difgrace.

" Methinks I fee the judges fet,
  " The council all attend,
" And JEMMY trembling at the bar,
  "Bereft of every friend.

" How fhall a mother's eye fuftain
  " The dreadful fight to fee!——
" Return, return, my haplefs fpoufe,
  " And leave the tafk to me."

* This little Poem was occafioned by the following fact:——A poft-boy was apprehended on fufpicion of ftealing a bank-note from a letter, which the author, at the requeft of a friend, had conveyed to the poft-office. This circumftance obliged her to appear as an evidence againft the unfortunate young man, where fhe was witnefs to the diftrefs of his aged parents, who were waiting at the door of the Hall, to learn the event of a trial which was to decide on the life of an only fon. The innocence of his intentions appearing very evident, the youth was acquitted.

' Perfuade me not, my faithful love,
   ' Perfuade me not to go,
' But let me fee my JEMMY's face,
   ' And fhare in all his woe.

' I'll kneel before his judge's feet,
   ' And prayers and tears employ—
' For pity take my wretched life,
   ' But fpare my darling boy.

' When trembling, proftrate in the duft,
   ' My heartfelt forrows flow,
' Sure, fure, the hardeft heart will melt
   ' To fee a mother's woe.

' How did I watch his infant years,
   ' Through fond affection blind,
' And hop'd the comfort of my age
   ' In JEMMY's love to find!

' Oft when he join'd the youthful train,
   ' And rov'd the woods among,
' Full many a wifhful look I fent,
   ' And thought he ftaid too long.

' And when at length I faw my boy
   ' Come bounding o'er the plain,
(' The fprightlieft of the fprightly throng,
   ' The foremoft of the train)

' How have I gaz'd with fond delight,
  ' His harmless joy to fee,
' As home he brought a load of flow'rs,
  ' And chofe the beft for me.

' Why would'ft thou feek the noify town,
 · ' Where fraud and cunning dwell?—
' Alas! the heart that knows no guile
  ' Should choofe the humble cell.

' So might I ftill with eager joy
  ' Expect my child's return;
' And not as now his haplefs fate
  ' In bitter forrow mourn.

' Laft night when all was dark and ftill,
  (' O wond'rous tale to tell!)
' I heard a mournful folemn found—
  ' Methought 'twas JEMMY's knell.

' And oft amidft the dreary gloom
  ' I heard a difmal groan—
' And oft I felt a clay-cold hand,
  ' Which fondly prefs'd my own.

' Anon I heard the found confus'd
  ' Of all the ruftick train,
' And JEMMY's fainting, trembling voice
  ' For pity begg'd in vain.

' Methought I faw the fatal cord,
  ' I faw him dragg'd along—
' I faw him feiz'd'——She could no more,
  For anguifh ftopp'd her tongue.

Her faithful partner gently ftrove
  Her finking heart to cheer,
Yet while his lips of comfort fpoke,
  He could not hide a tear.

But now the voice of joy or woe
  To her alike was vain;
Her thought ftill dwelt on JEMMY's fate,
  Her lips on JEMMY's name.

Thus on the mournful pair advanc'd,
  And reach'd the fatal place,
Where thoughtlefs crowds were gather'd round
  To fee their child's difgrace:——

Such crowds as run with idle gaze
  Alike to every fhew,
Nor heed a wretched father's tears,
  Nor feel a mother's woe.——

Sudden fhe ftopp'd—for now in view
  The crowded hall appear'd—
Chill horror feiz'd her ftiffen'd frame,
  Her voice no more was heard.

She could not move, fhe could not weep,
  Her hands were clafp'd on high;
And all her foul in eager gaze
  Seem'd ftarting from her eye.

For her the hufband trembled now
  With tender anxious fear;
" O Lucy! turn and fpeak to me:"
  But Lucy could not hear.

Still fix'd fhe ftood in filent woe,
  Still gazing on the door;
When lo! a murmur through the crowd
  Proclaim'd the trial o'er.

At once the blood forfook her cheek,
  Her feeble fpirits fled;
When Jemmy flew into her arms,
  And rais'd her drooping head.

The well-known voice recall'd her foul,
  She clafp'd him to her breaft:——
O joy too vaft for words to tell!
  Let Fancy paint the reft.

====

SUBJECT

L O V E

FOR THE VASE AT BATHEASTON VILLA.

====

WITH bow unftrung, and arrows broke,
 Young CUPID to his mother ran,
And tears faft flowing as he fpoke,
 He thus his fad complaint began:——

" Ah! where is now that boafted pow'r
 " Which kings and heroes once confefs'd?
" I try my arrows o'er and o'er,
 " But find they cannot reach the breaft.

" I feek the rooms, the play, the ball,
 " Where Beauty fpreads her brighteft charms;
" But loft in crowds my arrows fall,
 " And Pleafure flights my feeble arms.

" Yet real pleafure is not there,
 " A phantom ftill deludes their aim;
" In Diffipation's carelefs air
 " They feek her charms, but feek in vain.

C

" Here Pride eſſays my darts to throw,
    " But from her hand they ne'er can harm,
" For ſtill ſhe turns aſide the blow;
    " Not Beauty's ſelf with Pride can charm.

" Coquetry here with roving eyes
    " Quick darts a thouſand arrows round;
" She thinks to conquer by ſurprize—
    " But ah! thoſe arrows never wound.

" Here Cunning boaſts to guide their courſe
    " With cautious aim and ſly deſign;
" But ſtill ſhe checks their native force—
    " Touch'd by her hand, they drop from mine.

" Here Affectation taints the ſmile,
    " Which elſe had darted Love around:
" The charms of Art can ne'er beguile:
    " But where ſhall Nature's charms be found?

" While theſe their various arts eſſay,
    " And vainly ſtrive to gain the heart,
" Good-Senſe diſdainful turns away,
    " And Reaſon ſcorns my pointleſs dart.

" Yet they to Love were once ally'd,
    " For Love could ev'ry joy diſpenſe;
" Sweet Pleaſure ſmil'd by Virtue's ſide,
    " And Love was pair'd with Innocence."

Fair Venus clafp'd her darling child,
　　And gently footh'd his anxious breaft:
' Refume thy darts,' fhe faid, and fmil'd,
　　' Thy wrongs fhall quickly be redrefs'd.

' With artlefs blufh and gentle mien,
　　' With charms unknowing pride or care,
' With all the graces in her train,
　　' My lovely Anna* fhall appear.

' Go then, my boy, to earth again,
　　' Once more affume defpotic pow'r;
' For Modefty with her fhall reign,
　　' And Senfe and Reafon fhall-adore.'

---

* Mifs Anne M——ll, now Mrs. D——n.

TO

MISS ———,

THEN TWO YEARS OLD.

SWEET bloſſom, opening to the beams of day!
　Dear object of affection's tender care!
For whom ſhe gently ſmooths the painful way,
　Inſpires the anxious wiſh, the ardent pray'r!

How pleaſing in thy infant mind to trace
　The dawn of reaſon's force, of fancy's fire,
The ſoft impreſſion of each future grace,
　And all a parent's warmeſt hopes deſire!

How ſweet that ſmile, unknown to ev'ry art,
　Inſpir'd by innocence, and peace, and joy!
How pure the tranſports of thy guiltleſs heart,
　Which yet no fears alarm, no cares annoy.

No airy phantoms of uncertain woe,
　The bleſſings of the preſent hour allay;
No empty hopes a fancied good beſtow,
　Then leave the ſoul to real grief a prey.

Gay pleasure sparkles in thy gentle eye,
  Some new delight in every scene appears;
Yet soft affection heaves a secret sigh,
  And sends an anxious look to distant years.

While those dear smiles with tender love I view,
  And o'er thy infant charms enraptur'd bend,
Does my fond hope a real good pursue?
  And do these arms embrace a future friend?

Should heaven to me a lengthen'd date assign,
  Will e'er that love thy gentle heart engage
With friendship's purest flame to answer mine,
  And charm the languor of declining age?

Yet not for me these ardent wishes rise;
  Beyond the limits of my fleeting years,
For thee, dear babe, my prayers ascend the skies,
  And pleasing hope my anxious bosom cheers.

May innocence still guard thy artless youth,
  Ere vice and folly's snares thy breast alarm,
While sweetness, modesty, and spotless truth,
  Beam from thy soul, and brighten ev'ry charm!

May Heaven to thee its choicest gifts impart,
  Beyond what wealth bestows, or pride pursues;
With ev'ry virtue animate thy heart,
  And raise thy efforts to the noblest views.

In tranſport wrapt may each fond parent ſee
   Through riſing years thoſe virtues ſtill improve,
While every tender care now felt for thee,
   Thy heart repays with never-ceaſing love.

When pleaſure ſmiles, and·ſtrews thy path with flow'rs,
   And youthful fancy doubles every joy,
May brighter hopes attend thy gayeſt hours,
   And point to bliſs which time can ne'er deſtroy!

And when the pangs of woe thy breaſt muſt tear,
   When pleaſure fades, and fancy charms no more,
Still may thoſe hopes the gloomy proſpect cheer,
   Unmov'd by grief, unchang'd by fortune's pow'r.

May love, eſteem, and friendſhip, crown thy days,
   With joys to guilt unknown, from doubt ſecure,
While heavenly truth inſpires the voice of praiſe,
   And bids that praiſe beyond the world endure!

Through life to virtue's ſacred dictates true,
   Be ſuch thy joys as angels muſt approve,
Such as may lead to raptures ever new,
   To endleſs peace, and pureſt bliſs above.

L O U I S A.

A TALE.

" O LEND your wings, ye fav'ring gales,
    " And gently wave the fea,
" And fwell my hufband's fpreading fails,
    " And waft him home to me!

" His toils and dangers all are paft,
    " And bleft with fortune's ftore,
" From diftant climes he comes at laft
    " To view his native fhore.

" And with him comes the faithful youth,
    " Who gain'd my daughter's love;
" Whofe virtue, conftancy, and truth,
    " The coldeft heart might move.

" May all the graces wait around,
    " And heighten all her charms!——
" He comes, with wealth and glory crown'd,
    " To my LOUISA's arms.

" Now Fancy flies to diſtant days,
 " And views the lovely pair,
" And hears the voice of general praiſe
 " Their matchleſs worth declare.

" How ſhall thy mother's heart expand
 " With joys unknown before,
" When thouſands bleſs the bounteous hand
 " That gave thee wealth and pow'r!

" Do I not ſee a diſtant ſail
 " O'er yonder waves appear?—
" Our ardent vows at length prevail,
 " My heart proclaims them near.

" With us in every joy to ſhare,
 " Our much-loved heroes come—
" Propitious Heaven, O hear our pray'r!'
 " And guide them ſafely home!"

' Propitious Heaven, O hear our pray'r!'
 Louisa trembling cry'd,
For ah! the chill blaſt waved her hair,
 The riſing cloud ſhe ſpy'd.

Near and more near the tempeſt drew,
 The clouds obſcur'd the ſky,
The winds in hoarſer murmurs blew,
 The waves were toſs'd on high:

And now they dafh againft the fhore,
  And fhake the folid ground;
The thunder rolls, the torrents roar,
  The lightnings flafh around.——

Ah! who can paint LOUISA's fear,
  Her agonies impart?——
The fhrieks of death affail her ear,
  And horror chills her heart.

At length, the raging tempeft o'er,
  She view'd the fatal coaft;
A wreck appear'd upon the fhore—
  She funk—in terror loft.

" My life! my joy! my only love!"
  A voice at diftance cries:—
That voice her inmoft foul could move.
  She ftarts with wild furprife.

Now o'er the beach with eager hafte
  She fees her HENRY fly:
No more fhe feels her terrors paft:
  'Twas blifs—'twas extacy!

Her aged father too appears,
  He prefs'd her to his heart;
But, as he prefs'd, his ftreaming tears
  Some fecret grief impart.

His much-lov'd wife in tranſport flies,
　　In all their joy to ſhare;
Yet views her lord with anxious eyes,
　　And feels a tender fear.

The fond embrace he oft renews,
　　And oft, with grief oppreſs'd,
The fatal wreck again he views,
　　And ſmites his trembling breaſt.

" Lo! there," he cry'd, " the ſad remains
　" Of my once boaſted ſtore,
" For all the fruit of all our pains
　" Is ſunk—to riſe no more.

" Yet ſhould this breaſt ne'er heave a groan
　" For all my fruitleſs care:
" Did ſorrow ſeize on me alone,
　" My woes I well could bear:

" But ah! for thee my heart muſt grieve,
　" For thee I priz'd my gain:—
" And did I then my child deceive
　" With hopes believed in vain?

" Still to our humble home confin'd,
　" Muſt rural taſks employ
" A nymph to ſhine in courts deſign'd,
　" And brighten ev'ry joy.

" In thought, by pleafing hope infpir'd,
     " I faw my child appear,
" By all belov'd, by all admir'd,
     " The faireft of the fair.

" I faw her rais'd to pomp and ftate,
     " And, rich in fortune's ftore,
" I heard the praifes of the great,
     " The bleffings of the poor.

" With fond delight my bofom glow'd,
     " By foothing fancy led,
" And Heaven the wifh'd fuccefs beftow'd:—
     " But ah! the dream is fled.

" And thou, dear partner of each care,
     " This anxious heart has known;
" Thou too, with me, haft felt thy fhare
     " Of hopes—for ever gone.

" Thy thoughts, like mine, in time to come,
     " A fcene of blifs enjoy'd,
" Till one fad moment's fatal doom
     " The airy good deftroy'd.

" And thou with me our lofs muft mourn,
     " Thy tears with mine defcend;
" And thus, alas! my wifh'd return
     " Our tranfient joy muft end."

While thus with agonizing fighs
  They view'd the fatal place,
Louisa's mild, yet ftedfaft eyes
  Were fix'd on Henry's face.

By her own heart, his heart fhe knew,
  She read his virtues there:
Ah! bleft indeed the chofen few
  Who thus each thought can fhare!

Serene and firm their joys fhall prove,
  And every change endure,
No mean fufpicion taint their love,
  In juft efteem fecure.

And now her foul with tranfport glows,
  And animates each grace,
A fmile, beyond what pleafure knows,
  Adorns her lovely face.

‘ And is it thus, my friends,’ fhe cry'd,
  ‘ When every ftorm is paft,
‘ When all our fears at once fubfide,
  ‘ Thus do we meet at laft?

‘ O lift with me your hearts to Heaven
  ‘ In ftrains of ardent praife,
‘ With tranfport own the bleffings giv'n,
  ‘ To crown our future days.

' How oft my fervent pray'rs arofe,
  ' While terrors fhook my foul,
' To HIM who could the ftorm compofe,
  ' And winds and waves controul!

' My prayers are heard—my fears are gone,
  ' My much-lov'd friends I fee,
' I feel a joy till now unknown,—
  ' And can ye grieve for me?

' Content I fhar'd an humble fate,
  ' Nor wifh'd in courts to fhine;—
' The airy dream which pleas'd of late
  ' With joy I now refign.

' What though no fcenes of gay delight
  ' Amufe each idle gueft,
' Nor coftly luxuries invite
  ' To fhare the fplendid feaft!

' Yet Peace and Innocence fhall fmile,
  ' And purer joys afford,
' And Love, fecure from doubt or guile,
  ' Shall blefs our humble board.

' What though we boaft nor wealth, nor pow'r,
  ' Each forrow to relieve,
' A little, from our little ftore,
  ' The poor fhall yet receive:

' And words of peace fhall footh the woe
　' Which riches could not heal,
' And fweet Benevolence beftow
　' An aid which all muft feel.

' Beyond the reach of fortune's pow'r
　' Her gentle force extends,
' She cheers affliction's darkeft hour,
　' And joy her fteps attends.

' Though here to narrow bounds confin'd,
　' Ordain'd to lowly views,
' For ever free, the virtuous mind
　' Her glorious path purfues;

' In profp'rous ftate, o'er all fhe fhow'rs
　' The various bleffings given;
' In humble life, exerts her pow'rs,
　' And trufts the reft to Heav'n.

' The lofty dwellings of the great
　' Full many a wretch contain,
' Who feels the cares of pomp and ftate,
　' But feeks their joys in vain:

' Yet ftarting from his fhort repofe,
　' Alarm'd at ev'ry blaft,
' With anxious fear he dreads to lofe
　' That good he ne'er could tafte.

‘ And oft beneath the filent fhade
  ‘ A noble heart remains,
‘ Where Heaven’s bright image is difplay’d,
  ‘ And ev’ry virtue reigns.

‘ Sweet peace and joy that heart fhall find,
  ‘ Unmov’d by grief or pain :——
‘ Be fuch the lot to us affign’d,
  ‘ And fortune’s frowns are vain.——

‘ O ye, who taught me firft to know
  ‘ Bright Virtue’s facred flame,
To whom far more than life I owe,
  ‘ Who more than duty claim; •

‘ Ah! let me dry each tender tear,
  ‘ And ev’ry doubt deftroy,
‘ Difpel at once each anxious fear,
  ‘ And call you back to joy.

‘ And thou, my Henry! dearer far
  ‘ Than fortune’s richeft prize,
‘ I know thy heart——and thou canft dare
  ‘ Her treafures to defpife:

‘ A purer blifs that heart fhall prove
  ‘ From care and forrow free,
‘ Content with innocence and love,
  ‘ With poverty and me.’——
D

In tranſport loſt, and freed from fears,
    The happy parents ſmil'd,
And bluſhing dry'd the falling tears,
    And claſp'd their matchleſs child.

Her HENRY, fix'd in ſilent gaze,
    Beheld his lovely bride:
" O Heav'n! accept my humble praiſe,"
    At length entranc'd he cry'd.

" To all my ſtorms and dangers paſt,
    " If joys like theſe ſucceed,
" My utmoſt wiſh is crown'd at laſt,
    " And I am rich indeed.

" Then riſe, ye raging tempeſts! riſe,
    " And fortune's gifts deſtroy ;—
" Thy HENRY gains the nobleſt prize,
    " He feels the pureſt joy.

" Extatic bliſs his heart ſhall prove,
    " From care and ſorrow free,
" While bleſt with Innocence and Love,
    " With boundleſs wealth—in thee.

" Sweet Hope o'er every morn ſhall ſhed
    " Her ſoul-enliv'ning ray;
" Celeſtial Peace, by virtue led,
    " Shall cheer each cloſing day.

" Far from ambition's train remov'd,
  " And pleaſure's giddy throng, .
" Our blamelefs hours, by Heaven approv'd,
  " Shall gently glide along.

" O may I catch that facred fire
  " Which animates thy breaſt;
" Like thee to nobleſt heights afpire,
  " Like thee be truly bleſt!

" Thus ſhall the pleaſing charm of love
  " Bright virtue's force increafe—
" Thus every changing fcene ſhall prove
  " The road to laſting peace.

" And thus, thro' life, our hearts ſhall know
  " A more than mortal joy,
" Beyond what fortune can beſtow,
  " Or time, or death, deſtroy."

ENVY, A FRAGMENT.

ARGUMENT.

ENVY, *her character; her dwelling near the road that leads to the Temple of* VIRTUE. *A fruit-tree gives shelter and refreshment to travellers; she tears all the buds to prevent it, &c. A lamb takes shelter from the snow in her hut; she tears down the roof that it may not protect him, and leaves it so that none may ever find shelter there. Disturbs all travellers. Schemes laid to defeat her. Nothing will do but the shield of* TRUTH, *which is so bright that none dare carry it, because they cannot themselves stand it. At last* INNOCENCE, *attended by* MODESTY, *undertakes it.* ENVY *attacks them with fury, and throws a dart, which, instead of hurting, only strikes off the veil which hid the face of* MODESTY, *and makes all the world admire her.* ENVY *blushes for the first time.* INNOCENCE *holds up the shield.* ENVY *is dazzled, and becomes almost blind; she flies from them, and wanders about the world, trying to hurt every body, but being too blind to direct her darts, though they sometimes do harm, yet they always recoil upon herself, and give her the severest wounds.*

ENVY,

A FRAGMENT.

I.

Y E pleafing dreams of heavenly Poefy,
Which oft have footh'd my throbbing heart to reft,
And in foft ftrains of fweeteft minftrelfy
Have lull'd the tumults of this anxious breaft,
Or charm'd my foul with pleafures unpoffefs'd:
How fweet with you to wander all the day
In airy fcenes, by Fancy's pencil drefs'd,
To trace the windings of her devious way,
To feel her magic force, and own her boundlefs fway.

II.

See at her call the awful forms arife
Of ancient heroes, moulder'd in the tomb;
Again Vice trembles through her deep difguife,
And Virtue triumphs in a dungeon's gloom,
Or fmiles undaunted at a tyrant's doom.
Again fhe waves on high her magic wand——
The faded glories rife of Greece and Rome,
The heavenly Mufes lead a tuneful band,
And Freedom's fearlefs fons unnumber'd hofts with-
    ftand.

III.

And now to fofter fcenes my fteps fhe leads,
The fweet retreats of Innocence and Love,
Where frefheft flow'rets deck th' enamell'd meads,
And Nature's mufic warbles through the grove;
'Mongft rocks and caverns now fhe loves to rove,
And mark the torrents tumbling from on high,
And now fhe foars on daring wings, above
The vaft expanfe of yon ethereal fky,
Or darts through diftant time and long futurity.

IV.

And oft, when weary nature finks opprefs'd
Beneath the load of ficknefs and of pain,
When fweeteft mufic cannot lull to reft,
And prefent pleafure fpreads her charms in vain,
Bright Fancy comes, and burfts the mental chain,
And bears the foul on airy wings away;
Well pleas'd it wanders o'er her golden reign,
Enjoys the tranfports of fome diftant day,
And Pain's fufpended force a moment owns her fway.

V.

Ev'n in the lonelieft wild, the deepeft fhade,
Remote from ev'ry pleafing, focial fcene,
New wonders rife, by Fancy's pow'r difplay'd:
She paints each heavenly grace with gentle mein,
Celeftial Truth, and Innocence ferene,

And Hope, exulting ſtill in future joy,
Though dangers threat and tempeſts intervene;
And Patience, ever calm, though cares annoy,
And ſweet Benevolence, whoſe pleaſures ne'er can
   cloy.

VI.

In dangers firm, in triumphs ever mild,
The awful form of Fortitude appears;
Pure Joy, of heavenly Piety the child,
Serenely ſmiles, unmov'd by grief or fears;
Soft Mercy dries affliction's bitter tears,   `
Still bleſt in ev'ry bleſſing ſhe beſtows;
While Friendſhip's gentle voice each ſorrow cheers:
Sweet are her joys, and pleaſing ev'n her woes,
When warm'd by Virtue's fire the ſacred ardour glows.

VII.

Thus Fancy's pow'r in ſolitude can charm,
Can rouſe each latent virtue in the heart,
Preſerve the heavenly ſpark for ever warm,
And guiltleſs pleaſures ev'ry hour impart.
Yet oh! beware—leſt Vice with fatal art
Should taint the gift for Virtue's aid deſign'd;
Leſt Fancy's ſting ſhould point affliction's dart,
Or empty ſhadows check th' aſpiring mind,
By vain delights ſubdu'd, or vainer fears confin'd.

VIII.

For oft when Virtue prompts the gen'rous deed,
And points the way to gain the glorious prize,
Imagin'd ills her upward flight impede,
And all around fantaſtic terrors riſe:
Ev'n Vice itſelf can Fancy's pow'r diſguiſe
With borrow'd charms, enchanting to betray:
Oh! then let Reaſon watch with cautious eyes,
Secure its active force in Virtue's way,
Then ſlack the rein at will, and free let Fancy ſtray.

IX.

Thus muſing late at evening's ſilent hour,
My wand'ring footſteps ſought the lonely ſhade;
And gently led by Fancy's magic pow'r,
Methought at once, to diſtant realms convey'd,
New ſcenes appear'd, by mortal ne'er ſurvey'd;
Such as were fabled erſt in fairy land,
Where elfin Knights their proweſs oft diſplayed,
And mighty Love inſpir'd the warlike band
To ſeek adventures hard at Beauty's high command.

X.

Full many a path there was on ev'ry ſide,
Theſe waſte and wild, and thoſe beſet with flow'rs;
Where many a pilgrim wander'd far and wide,
Some bent to ſeek gay Pleaſure's roſy bow'rs,
And ſome to gain Ambition's lofty tow'rs:

While others view their labours with difdain,
And prize alone the gifts which Fortune fhow'rs;
With carelefs fteps fome wander o'er the plain,
And fome with ardour ftrive bright Virtue's hill
    to gain.

XI.

But many foes in ev'ry path were feen.
Who ftrove by ev'ry art to ftop the way:
Here Indolence appear'd with vacant mein,
And painted forms of terror and difmay;
And there the Paffions rofe in dread array,
And fill'd with clouds and darknefs all the air;
While empty fears and hopes alike betray,
And Pride, with Folly join'd, deftructive pair!
Drew many from each path, then left them to defpair.

XII.

Yet ftill diftinguifh'd o'er the hoftile band,
By all detefted, and to all a foe,
Pale ENVY rofe: while, trembling in her hand,
Her poifon'd fhaft ftill aim'd fome deadly blow,
Her eyes ftill wander'd in purfuit of woe:
For her, in vain rifes the cheerful morn,
In vain the flow'rs with frefheft luftre glow,
Vain all the charms which Nature's face adorn:
They cannot cheer a heart with ceafelefs anguifh torn.

XIII.

Befide the way that leads to Virtue's fhrine,
This wicked hag her fav'rite dwelling chofe,
Around her walls did baneful nightfhade twine,
And twifted thorns did all her hut compofe;
And ftill from morning's dawn to ev'ning's clofe,
Some horrid purpofe would her thoughts employ;
For never could her heart enjoy repofe,
Nor e'er her reftlefs fpirit tafte of joy,
Save when her cruel arts could other's peace deftroy.

XIV.

The fprightly voice of guiltlefs Pleafure's train,
The pleafing fmile which Peace and Virtue wear,
Whofe gentle force might charm the fenfe of pain,
Sufpend diftrefs, and fmooth the brow of care,
Still with new pangs her cruel heart would tear:
But when fhe heard Affliction's bitter cries,
Or view'd the horrid form of dark Defpair,
A tranfient gladnefs lighten'd in her eyes—
But tranfient ftill and vain are ENVY's wretched joys.

* * * * * * *

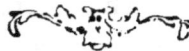

NEW YEAR.

'TIS paſt:—another year for ever gone
Proclaims the end of all;—with awful voice
It calls the ſoul to thought.   Awhile ſhe turns
From preſent ſcenes, and wanders o'er the paſt;
Or, darting forward, ſtrives to pierce the veil
Which hides from mortal eyes the time to come.

O Thou, to grateful mem'ry ever dear!
Whom fond affection ſtill delights to name!
Whom ſtill my heart exults to call ' My Friend!'
In fancy yet be preſent.——Oft with Thee
In many a lonely walk and ſilent ſhade
My ſoul holds converſe!—oft recalls the hours
When pleas'd attention hung upon thy voice,
While the pure dictates of celeſtial Truth
In Friendſhip's gentleſt accents charm'd my ear,
And ſooth'd each anxious thought, and ſhew'd the way
Which leads to preſent peace and future bliſs:—
Though now far diſtant, yet in thought be near,
And ſhare with me Reflection's ſacred hour.

And oh! to Thee may each revolving year
Its choiceſt bleſſings bring! May Heavenly Peace,
To every thoughtleſs mind unknown—purſued
In vain through ſcenes of viſionary good—
That peace which dwells with piety alone,
Still on thy ſteps through every ſtage attend!
And pureſt joy from Virtue's ſacred ſource,
Bleſt in the thought of many a well-ſpent day,
Bleſt in the proſpect of unbounded bliſs,
Cheer every hour, and triumph in the laſt!

As when a traveller, who long has rov'd
Through many a varied path, at length attains
Some eminence, from whence he views the land
Which late he paſs'd—groves, ſtreams, and lawns appear,
And hills with flocks adorn'd, and lofty woods;
And ev'ry charm which Nature's hand beſtows
In rich profuſion decks the ſmiling ſcene—
No more he views the rugged thorny way,
The ſteep aſcent, the ſlippery path, which led
High o'er the brink of ſome rude precipice;
Unnumber'd beauties, ſcarce obſerv'd before,
At once combine to charm his raptur'd view,
And backward turning, oft in tranſport loſt,
His toils and dangers paſt no more are felt,
But long and tedious ſeems the road to come :——
Thus oft, when youth is fled, when health decays,
And cares perplex, and trifling pleaſures cloy;

Sick of vain hopes and tir'd of prefent fcenes,
The foul returns to joys fhe feels no more,
And backward cafts her view.   Then Fancy comes
In Memory's form, and gilds the long-paft days,
Recalls the faded images of joy,
Paints every happy moment happier ftill;
But hides each anxious fear, and heartfelt pang,
Each pleafure loft, and hope purfued in vain,
Which oft o'erfpread with gloom the gayeft hour,
And taught ev'n Youth and Innocence to mourn.

   O Happinefs, in every varied fcene,
Thro' toil, thro' danger, and thro' pain purfued!
Yet oft when prefent fcarce enjoy'd,—when paft,
Recall'd to wound the heart, to blaft the fweets
Yet given to life :——How are thy votaries,
Mifled by vain delufions, thus deceiv'd?
Let rifing Hope, for ever on the wing,
Still point to diftant good, to perfect blifs;
While confcious of fuperior pow'rs, the foul
Exulting hears her call, and longs to foar
To fcenes of real and unfading joy.
Yet while on earth fome feeble rays are fhed
To cheer the mournful gloom:—oh ! let not man
Reject the proffer'd gift!—With innocence
And gratitude enjoy'd, each prefent good
Beyond the fleeting moment may extend
Its pleafing force.——When Nature's varied charms,

In all the gayeſt luſtre of the ſpring,
Delight the wond'ring view!—while every grove
With artleſs muſic hails the riſing morn,
The ſportive lambkins play, the ſhepherd ſings,
Creation ſmiles, and every boſom feels
The general joy;—oh! ſay, from ſcenes like theſe
Shall not the ſweet impreſſions ſtill remain
Of Innocence and Peace, and ſocial Love,
To bleſs the future hour?—When the glad heart
Exulting beats at Friendſhip's ſacred call,
And feels what language never can expreſs:
While every joy exalted and refin'd,
And each tumultuous paſſion charm'd to peace,
Own the ſweet influence of its matchleſs power;
(That power which ev'n o'er grief itſelf can ſhed
A heavenly beam, when pleaſure courts in vain,
And wealth and honours paſs unheeded by:)
Shall joys like theſe, on Virtue's baſis rais'd,]
Like Fancy's vain deluſions paſs away?
Oh, no!—Nor time, nor abſence, ſhall efface
The ever dear remembrance; ev'n when paſt,
When deep affliction mourns the bleſſing gone,
Yet ſhall that bleſſing be for ever priz'd,
For ever felt.——When heaven-born Charity
Expands the heart, and prompts the liberal hand
To ſooth diſtreſs, ſupply the various wants
Of friendleſs poverty, and dry the tears
Which bathe the widow's cheek, whoſe deareſt hope

Is fnatch'd away, and helplefs orphans afk
That aid fhe cannot give :—Say, fhall the joy
(Pure as the facred fource from whence it fprings)
Which then exalts the foul, fhall *this* expire?——
The grafs fhall wither, and the flower fhall fade,
But Heaven's eternal Word fhall ftill remain,
And Heaven's eternal Word pronounc'd it bleft.

Ye calm delights of Innocence and Peace!
Ye joys by Virtue taught, by Heaven approv'd!
Is there a heart, which, loft in felfifh views,
Ne'er felt your pleafing force, ne'er knew to fhare
Another's joy, or heave a tender figh
For forrows not its own;—which all around
Beholds a dreary void, where Hope perhaps
May dart a feeble ray, but knows not where
To point its aim? (For real good, unknown
While prefent, is purfued, but ne'er attain'd)
Is there a heart like this? At fuch a fight,
Let foft Compaffion drop a filent tear,
And Charity reluctant turn away
From woes fhe ne'er fhall feel, nor can relieve.
But oh! let thofe whom Heaven has taught to feel
The pureft joys which mortals e'er can know,
With gratitude recall the bleffings given,
Though grief fucceed; nor e'er with envy view
That calm which cold indifference feems to fhare,

F.

And think thofe happy who can never lofe
That good they never knew:—for joys like thefe
Refine, ennoble, elevate the mind;
And never, never, fhall fucceeding woes
Efface the bleft impreffion:—Grief itfelf
Retains it ftill; while Hope exulting comes
To fnatch them from the power of time and death,
And tell the foul—*They never fhall decay.*

When Youth and Pleafure gild the fmiling morn,
And Fancy fcatters rofes all around,
What blifsful vifions rife! In profpect bright
Awhile they charm the foul: but fcarce attain'd,
The gay delufion fades.——Another comes,
The foft enchantment is again renew'd,
And Youth again enjoys the airy dreams
Of fancied good.——But ah! how oft ev'n thefe
By ftern Affliction's hand are fnatch'd away,
Ere yet experience proves them vain, and fhews
That earthly pleafures to a heavenly mind
Are but the fhadows of fubftantial blifs!
But Pleafure rais'd by Virtue's powerful charm,
Above each tranfient view, each meaner aim,
Can blefs the prefent hour, and lead the foul
To brighter profpects, rich in every good
Which man can feel, or Heaven itfelf beftow.

While thus returning o'er the long-paſt ſcenes
Of former life, the mind recalls to view
The ſtrange viciſſitudes of grief and joy,
O may the grateful heart for ever own
The various bleſſings given! nor dare repine
At ills which all muſt ſhare; or deem thoſe ills
From Chance or Fate (thoſe empty names which veil
The ignorance of man) could ever flow;
But warn'd alike by Pleaſure and by Pain,
That higher joys await the virtuous mind
Than aught on earth can yield, in every change
Adore that Power which rules the whole, and gives,
In Pleaſure's charms, in Sorrow's keeneſt pangs,
The means of good, the hope—the pledge of bliſs.

Thou riſing year, now opening to my view,
Yet wrapp'd in darkneſs—whither doſt thou lead?
What is Futurity?——It is a time
When joys, unknown to former life, *may* ſhed
Their brighteſt beams on each ſucceeding day;
When Health again *may* bloom, and Pleaſure ſmile,
(By Pain no more allay'd) and new delights
On every changing ſeaſon ſtill attend;
Each morn returning wake the ſoul to joy
From balmy ſlumbers, undiſturb'd by care;
Succeſs ſtill wait on Hope; and every hour
In peace and pleaſure gently glide away.——
But ah! how rare on earth are years like this!

In the dark profpect of Futurity,
Far other fcenes than thefe may yet remain:
Affliction there may aim her keeneft fhafts
To tear the heart,—while pain and ficknefs wafte
The feeble frame by flow-confuming pangs,
And eafe and comfort loft are fought in vain;
For there, perhaps, no friendly voice may cheer
The tedious hours of grief, but all around
Expiring joys and blafted hopes appear,
New woes fucceed to woes, and every good
On earth be fnatched away.—How then fhall man
Salute the rifing year?—Shall cheerful Hope
Receive the welcome gueft; or Terror wait
In fpeechlefs anguifh the impending ftorm?—
Prefumptuous mortal, ceafe:—O turn thine eyes
On the dark manfions of the filent dead,
And check the bold enquiry;—never more
The rifing fun may fhed its beams on thee;
Perhaps, ev'n now, the fatal hour is come
Which ends at once thy earthly hopes and fears,
And feals thy doom through vaft eternity.—
How awful is the thought! and who fhall fay
It is not juft? What mortal fhall difclofe
The dark decrees of Heaven?——But grant, to life
A longer date affign'd, another year
On earth beftow'd; in deepeft fhades conceal'd
Its good or ill remains; no mortal hand
Can draw the veil which hides it from thy view.

Hence then, ye airy dreams by fancy led!
Vain hopes, and vainer fears—deceive no more!
In native luftre bright let Truth appear,
With her pure beams illume the dark unknown,
And fhew what man of future days can know.

What is Futurity?——It is a time
By Heaven in mercy giv'n, where all may find
Their beft, their trueft good, the means, the power,
To elevate their nature, to exert
Each nobler faculty, and ftill to rife
In every virtue.——Here the beft may find
Improvement: for what mortal e'er attain'd
Perfection's utmoft point?—And here ev'n thofe,
Who long, by vice and folly led aftray,
Forfook the paths of wifdom and of truth,
May yet return, and with new ardour feek
That long-neglected good, which, though defpis'd,
Rejected once, may here be yet attain'd.——

Know then, whoe'er thou art, on whom high Heaven
Another year of life will now beftow,
That year may lead thee to eternal peace,
May cancel follies paft, redeem the time
In thoughtlefs diffipation once abus'd,
Difpel the fhades of vice, the gloom of care,
Call forth each latent virtue, and impart
New ftrength, new hopes, and joys which ne'er fhall fail.

Then hail, bright profpect of the rifing year!
The fchool of virtue, and the road to blifs!——
No more the fhades of doubt are fpread around;
No more ideal pleafures deck the fcene
With airy forms of good, which Fancy's felf
Scarce dares enjoy; no more by terror led
A train of woes in long fucceffion rife,
And deepeft horror o'er the time to come
Extends her baleful influence;—by the power
Of Truth fubdued, at once they difappear,
And furer hopes and brighter views arife,
Than Pleafure e'er could give, or Pain deftroy,
To chafe each vain delufion far away,
And fhew the glorious prize which future days
May yet attain:——This, this alone is fure:
The reft, involv'd in dark uncertainty,
But mocks our fearch:—But oh! how bleft the path
(Whate'er it be) which leads to endlefs reft!——

Then let Affliction come;—fhall man complain
Of feeming ills, which Heaven in mercy fends
To check his vain purfuits, exalt his views,
Improve his virtues, and direct the foul
To feek that aid which ne'er can fail, that aid
Which all who feek fhall find? Oh! in the hour
Of deepeft horror, when the throbbing heart,
Opprefs'd with anguifh, can fuftain no more,
May Patience ftill, and Refignation, come

To cheer the gloom!—not fuch as his who boaſts
Superior powers, a mind above the reach
Of human weakneſs, yet with ardour ſeeks
The frail ſupport of tranſitory praiſe;—
Or his, who trembling at an unknown power,
Submits in ſilence to Omnipotence,
And ſtruggling checks the murmurs of his breaſt;—
But that ſweet Peace, that heartfelt Confidence,
(By heavenly hope and filial love inſpir'd,
In Truth's inviolable word ſecure)
Which pain and ſorrow never can deſtroy;
Which ſmile triumphant in the gloom of woe,
And own a Father's pow'r, a Father's love
O'er all preſiding.——Bleſt in thoughts like theſe
The mourner's heart ſtill feels a ſecret joy,
Which pleaſure ne'er could yield:—no murmurs now
Diſturb its peace;—but every wiſh reſign'd
To Wiſdom, Power, and Goodneſs infinite,
Celeſtial hope and comfort beam around
O'er all the proſpect of ſucceeding time,
And never-fading glories cloſe the ſcene.

O Thou, great ſource of every good! by whom
This heart was taught to beat, theſe thoughts to range
O'er the wide circuit of the univerſe,
To ſoar beyond the fartheſt bounds of time,
And pant for bliſs which earth could ne'er beſtow;—
While worlds unnumber'd tremble at thy power,

And hofts celeftial own their loftieft ftrain
Too weak to tell thy praife;—O how fhall man
E'er lift his voice to Thee!——Yet at thy call
Thy fervant comes.   O hear my humble prayer:—
By thy Almighty power direct, fuftain
My feeble efforts; and whate'er the lot
To me on earth affign'd, O guide me ftill,
By the bleft light of thy eternal truth,
Through every varied fcene of joy or woe;
Support my weaknefs by thy mighty aid,
And lead my foul to Peace—to Blifs—to Thee!

ESSAYS.

ESSAYS.

====

ON

SENSIBILITY.

=========

IT is a common obfervation, that in this world we ftand more in need of comforts than of pleafures. Pain, ficknefs, loffes, difappointments, forrows of every kind, are fown fo thick in the path of life, that thofe who have attempted to teach the way to be happy, have in general beftowed more attention on the means of fupporting evil, than of feeking good;—nay, many have gone fo far as to recommend infenfibility as the moft defirable ftate of mind, upon a fuppofition, that evil (or the appearance of evil) fo far predominates, that the good, in general, is not fufficient to counterbalance it, and that therefore, by leffening the fenfe of both, we fhould be gainers on the whole, and might purchafe conftant eafe, and freedom from all anxiety, by giving up pleafures, which are always uncertain, and

often

often lead to the fevereft fufferings: and this, taking all circumftances together, it has been thought would be a defirable change.

On the fame principle, much ferious advice has been beftowed on the young, the gay, and the happy, to teach them—to be moderate in their purfuits and wifhes, that they may avoid the pangs of difappointment in cafe they fhould not fucceed;—to allay the pleafure they might receive from the enjoyment of every good they poffefs, by dwelling continually on the thought of its uncertainty;—to check the beft affections of their hearts, in order to fecure themfelves from the pain they may afterwards occafion;—in fhort, to deprive themfelves of the good they might enjoy, from a fear of the evil which may follow:—which is fomething like advifing a man to keep his eyes conftantly fhut, as the moft certain way to avoid the fight of any difagreeable object.

Thofe, on the other hand, who are in a ftate of affliction, are advifed to moderate their grief, by confidering, that they knew beforehand the uncertainty of every good they poffeffed;—that nothing has befallen them but what is the common lot of mankind;—that the evil confifts chiefly in the opinion they form of it;—that what is independent on themfelves, cannot

really

really touch them but by their own fault; and their concern cannot make things better than they are.

Many other confiderations of the fame kind are added, to which probably no person under the immediate influence of real affliction ever paid the leaft attention; and which, even if they are allowed their greateft force, could only filence complaints, and lead the mind into a ftate of infenfibility, but could never produce the fmalleft degree of comfort or of happinefs.

In order to determine whether this be really the way to pafs through life with the greateft eafe and fatisfaction, it may not be ufelefs to enquire in what ftate the mind of man would be, fuppofing it really to have attained that infenfibility, both as to pain and pleafure, which has been reprefented as fo defirable;— I fpeak of a mind poffeffed of its full powers and faculties, and capable of exerting them; for there may be fome who, from natural incapacity, or want of education, are really incapable of it, and can drudge on through life with fcarce any feelings or apprehenfions beyond the prefent moment:—But if thefe are fuppofed to be the happieft of mankind, then the end of the argument will be,

" In happinefs the beaft excels the man,
" The worm excels the beaft, the clod the worm."

And

And it feems fcarce poffible to fuppofe any rational creature (not under the immediate infiuence of paffion) to be really fo far convinced of this, as to wifh to exchange his fituation in the fcale of being with the beaft or the clod.

If then we fuppofe the mind in full poffeffion of its powers, is it poffible to fuppofe that the way to enjoy happinefs, or even peaee, is by preventing their exertion? If pofitive pain and pleafure are taken away, if all the objects propofed to it make no impreffion, will the mind therefore be at eafe? Far from it furely. On the eontrary, it will be torn in pieees by wifhes whieh will have no object whereon to fix ;—it will feel in itfelf powers and eapacities for happinefs : but finding nothing to make it happy, thofe very powers will make it miferable;—having no motive for action, no object to purfue, every rifing day will prefent a blank, which it will be impoffible to fill up with any thing that ean give pleafure; and the wifh of every morning will be, that the day were paft, though there be no profpect that the next will produce any thing more fatisfactory.

Could it be poffible for any perfon really to have attained to fuch a ftate as this, inftead of finding it a ftate of eafe and fatisfaction, we fhould fee him weary of himfelf and all around him, unhappy with nothing

to

to complain of, and without any hope of being ever otherwife, becaufe he would have no determinate wifh, in the accomplifhment of which he could promife himfelf any enjoyment.

But, happily for mankind, a ftate like this is not to be attained by any thinking perfon; and thofe who place their notion of happinefs in mere freedom from fuffering, muft be reduced to envy the happinefs of the beafts of the field;—for it is not the happinefs of man.

Thofe, indeed, who from a ftate of exceffive fuffering are fuddenly relieved, and reftored to eafe of body and mind, may, at the time, feel more joy from that eafe than they would have felt from the greateft pofitive pleafure; but then that joy will be tranfient indeed, fince it arifes only from a comparifon of paft fufferings, the fenfe of which is quickly loft; and as foon as the mind returns to its natural ftate, it feels again the want of that enjoyment for which it was formed, and becomes miferable, not from any pofitive fufferings, but merely from the want of happinefs.

Thofe who take pleafure in arguments which anfwer no other purpofe than to exercife their ingenuity, may amufe themfelves with difputing whether this inextinguifhable thirft after happinefs be really a defirable

gift,

gift, and whether it might not have been happier for man, to have been formed without that activity of mind which prompts him continually to feek for fome enjoyment. But to thofe who feel its force, it is furely a more important point to enquire how it may beft be fatisfied; and whether it may not be poffible to regulate thofe affections which they cannot fupprefs, and, by directing them to proper objects, to find in them a fource of happinefs, which, though it can neither prevent fufferings, nor take away the fenfe of them, may yet be felt at the fame time, and ferve in a great degree to counterbalance the effect of them.

It muft, I believe, be allowed, that every man, who reflects on his own fituation, will find that it has its pleafures and its pains,—unmixed happinefs or mifery not being the lot of this life, but referved for a future ftate. The happinefs of life muft then be eftimated by the proportion its joys bear to its forrows; and if what has been before fuppofed concerning the ftate of the mind be juft, he will not be found to be the happieft man who has the feweft forrows, but he whofe joys overbalance his forrows in the greateft degree.

This then fhould be our aim in the purfuit of happinefs:—not to conquer the fenfe of fuffering, for that is impoffible; not to fupprefs our defires and
hopes

hopes, for that (if it were poſſible) would only debaſe the mind, not make 'it happy; but to cultivate every faculty of the ſoul which may prove a ſource of innocent delight; to endeavour as far as poſſible to keep the mind open to a ſenſe of pleaſure, inſtead of ſullenly rejecting all, becauſe we cannot enjoy exactly what we wiſh;—above all, to ſecure to ourſelves a laſting fund of real pleaſures, which may compenſate thoſe afflictions they cannot prevent, and make us not inſenſible, but happy in the midſt of them.

It is very certain that nothing can fully do this, except Religion, and the glorious proſpects it offers to our hopes; this is the only foundation of laſting happineſs, the only ſource of never-failing comfort. While our beſt affections are fixed on any thing in this world, they muſt always give us pain, becauſe they will find nothing which can fully ſatisfy them; but when once they are fixed on Infinite Perfection, as their ultimate object, the ſubordinate exerciſes of them will furniſh many ſources of pleaſure and advantage, and ſhould be cultivated both with a view to preſent and future happineſs.

It ſeems ſtrange to obſerve, that there are few, if any, in the world, who enjoy all the bleſſings which are beſtowed upon them, and make their ſituation in

F

life as happy as it might be. Wherever the felfifh
paffions are indulged to excefs, this muft always be the
confequence; for none can be happy while they make
others miferable.

Whoever is poffeffed of any degree of power, from
the greateft monarch on the throne to the mafter of
the meaneft cottage, muft depend for his happinefs on
thofe over whom that power is exercifed; and whether
he will or no, muft fhare in the fufferings which he
inflicts, and feel the want of that fatisfaction which he
might have received from a different employment of
his power.

The truth of this obfervation has been experienced
by all who ever endeavoured to purchafe their own
happinefs at the expence of that of others. But even
where this is not the cafe, where the intentions are
good, and the pleafures of life are not embittered by
the fenfe of guilt, it often happens that difappointments bring on difguft; the pleafures which were expected are not found; and therefore thofe which might
be found, are undervalued;—the mind is diffatisfied,
and feeks for reafons to juftify itfelf for being fo; and
when forrows are fought for, it is not difficult to find
them.

Such

Such a difpofition can poifon every pleafure, and add numberlefs imaginary evils to thofe which muſt inevitably be met with in the path of life. By degrees the activity of the foul is loſt; every forrow appears infupportable; every difficulty unconquerable; no ob-ject is thought worth purfuing; and life itfelf becomes a burden.

To guard againſt the fatal effects which difappoint-ments are apt to have upon the mind, is a point of the utmoſt confequence towards pafling through life with any tolerable degree of comfort and fatisfaction; for difappointments, more or lefs, muſt be the lot of all.

At the firſt entrance into the world, when the ima-gination is active, the affections warm, and the heart a ftranger to deceit, and confequently to fufpicion, what delightful dreams of happinefs are formed! Whatever may be the object in which that happinefs is fuppofed to confiſt, that object is purfued with ardour;—the gay and thoughtlefs feek for it in diflipation and amufe-ment; the ambitious, in power, fame, and honours; the affectionate, in love and friendſhip: but how few are there who find in any of thefe objects that happi-nefs which they expected!

Pleafure,

Pleafure, fame, &c. even when they are in any degree obtained, ſtill leave a void in the ſoul, which continually reminds the poſſeſſor, that this is not the happineſs for which he was formed; and even the beſt affections are liable to numberleſs diſappointments, and often productive of the ſevereſt pangs.

The unſuſpecting heart forms attachments, before reaſon is capable of judging whether the objects of them are ſuch as are qualified to make it happy; and it often happens, that the fatal truth is not diſcovered till the affections are engaged too far to be recalled, and then the diſappointment muſt prove a laſting ſorrow.

But it is not neceſſary to enumerate the diſappointments which generally attend on the purſuits of youth; and indeed the proſpect is too painful to dwell upon: the intention of mentioning them is only to guard againſt the effects they may produce.

The imagination has painted an object, which perhaps is not to be found in this world; that object has been purſued in vain: but ſhall we therefore conclude, that no object is worth purſuing, and ſink into a liſtleſs, inactive ſtate, in which we muſt grow weary of ourſelves, and all the world?

The

The young are too apt to fancy that the affections of their hearts will prove the fource of nothing but pleafure;—thofe who are farther advanced in life, are much too apt to run into the contrary extreme. The error of the firft, even taking it in the worft light, is productive of fome pleafure as well as pain; that of the laft ferves only to throw a damp over every pleafure, and can be productive of nothing but pain. It leads indeed to the moft fatal confequences, fince it tends to make *felf* the only object; and the heart which is merely felfifh muft ever be incapable of virtue and of happinefs, and a ftranger to all the joys of affection and benevolence; without which the happieft ftate in this world muft be infipid, and which may prove the fource of many pleafures, even in the midft of the fevereft afflictions.

In every ftate of life, in fpite of every difappointment, *thofe* fhould ftill be cherifhed and encouraged; for though they may not always beftow fuch pleafures as the romantic imaginations of youth had painted, yet they will ftill beftow fuch as can be found in nothing elfe in this world; and indeed they are neceffary, in order to give a relifh to every·enjoyment.

I mention an affectionate and a benevolent difpofition together, becaufe I believe, when they are genuine,

F 3   they

they never can be feparated; and, perhaps, the difappointments fo often complained of may fometimes be
occafioned by a miftake upon this fubject; for there is
a felfifh attachment, which often ufurps the name
of friendfhip, though it is indeed fomething totally different.   It is an attachment like that which a mufician
feels for his inftrument, or a virtuofo for his pictures
and his ftatues;—the affection is not fixed on the object itfelf, but merely on the pleafure received from it.
Such an attachment as this is liable to numberlefs
little jealoufies and uneafineffes;—the fmalleft doubt
is fufficient to awaken its fears; the moft trifling
error excites its refentment, and that refentment is
immediately expreffed by complaints, and often by
upbraidings.

   True friendfhip is not indeed lefs quick-fighted; it
watches with a tender and anxious folicitude to promote the welfare and happinefs of the object which it
loves; it is a kind of microfcope which difcovers every
fpeck; but then the difcovery does not excite anger and
refentment, ftill lefs could it lead to unkindnefs and
upbraidings:—it infpires a concern like that which we
feel for our own errors and imperfections, and produces an earneft defire and fincere endeavour to remove
them.

                                                With

With fuch a friend, the heart may appear juft as it is, and enjoy the pleafure of an unbounded confidence; —but with thofe whofe affection is founded on a regard to themfelves, every word and action muft be weighed, and the fear of giving offence muft throw a reftraint over every converfation.

The real friend will be difpofed to love all thofe who are any way connected with the object of his affection; he will be fincerely interefted for their welfare, and will wifh to gain their affection, and promote their happinefs.

The felfifh will view them with a jealous eye, continually apprehenfive that they may rob him of fome part of a treafure which he would wifh to engrofs.

It would be eafy to carry on the contraft much farther; for indeed it might be fhewn in almoft every inftance. But what has been faid may be fufficient to fhew how very wide is the difference between that fort of attachment of which a felfifh heart is capable, and that which alone deferves the name of real friendfhip; though it is often too indifcriminately given to both: the one is an enemy to general benevolence; the other flows from the fame fource, and belongs to the fame character.

Such

Such a difpofition, it muft be allowed, may prove
the fource of many pleafures; but it may be objected,
that it will prove the fource of many forrows alfo: and
indeed, in this imperfect ftate, this truth is too certain
to be difputed. But if it can be proved, that on the
whole it affords more joys than forrows, that will be
fufficient to the prefent purpofe; if it be allowed that
the happinefs of man muft confift in pofitive enjoyment,
not in mere freedom from fuffering.

And furely much more than this might eafily be
proved, fince it not only can afford pleafures of the
moft exalted kind, and give new relifh to every other
pleafure; but even in the midft of the moft painful
fufferings it ever occafioned, it can at the fame time
infpire a fecret fatisfaction, of which thofe who never
felt it can hardly form any idea.

With fuch a difpofition, power and riches may be real
bleffings; fince they furnifh frequent opportunities of
beftowing happinefs, and confequently of enjoying it in
the higheft degree. But even without thefe advantages,
the truly benevolent, in whatever fituation in life they
may be placed, will find numberlefs fources of pleafure
and delight, which to others muft be for ever unknown.
All the happinefs they fee, becomes in fome fort their
own: and even, under the preffure of the greateft afflictions,

tions, they can rejoice at the good which others enjoy; and far from repining at the comparifon, they find in the thought of it a pleafure and fatisfaction, to which no fuffering of their own can render them infenfible; but which, on the contrary, prove a powerful cordial to help them to fupport thofe fufferings.

Even the face of inanimate nature fills them with a fatisfaction which the infenfible can never know, while they are warmed with gratitude to the Giver of every good, and joy at the thought that their fellow-creatures fhare thofe bleffings with them. They may even experience fomething like the pleafure of beftow-ing happinefs, while they rejoice in all that is be-ftowed, and feel in their hearts that they would beftow it if they could.

It is true indeed, that they muft fhare in the forrows of others, as well as in their joys; but then this may often lead to the heavenly pleafure of relieving them, if not as fully as they could wifh, yet at leaft in fome degree; for true benevolence can difcover numberlefs methods of relieving diftrefs, which would efcape the notice of the carelefs and infenfible. When relief is not in their power, fome expreffions of kindnefs, and the appearance of a defire to give comfort and affiftance, may at leaft contribute to foothe the wounded mind, and

and they may ftill enjoy the pleafure which attends on
every endeavour to do good, even on the unfuccefsful;
and when they are placed beyond the reach of this, and
can only offer up a fecret prayer for thofe whofe fufferings they cannot alleviate, even this will be attended
with a heartfelt fatisfaction, more than fufficient to
fupprefs every wifh that they could behold the forrows
of others with indifference, if it were poffible that fuch
a wifh could ever arife in a truly benevolent heart.

Such a difpofition will be a powerful prefervative
againft that wearinefs of mind, which is fo often an
attendant on what is generally efteemed a happy fituation in this world.

Thofe who are freed from cares and anxieties, who
are furrounded by all the means of enjoyment, and
whofe pleafures prefent themfelves without being
fought for, are often unhappy in the midft of all,
merely becaufe that activity of mind, in the proper
exercife of which our happinefs confifts, has in them
no object on which it may be employed. But when
the heart is fincerely and affectionately interefted for
the good of others, a new fcene of action is continually open, every moment may be employed in fome
pleafing and ufeful purfuit. New opportunities of
doing good are continually prefenting themfelves; new
                                                    fchemes

schemes are formed and ardently purfued; and even when they do not fucceed, though the difappointment may give pain, yet the pleafure of felf-approbation will remain; and the purfuit will be remembered with fatis-faction. The next opportunity which offers itfelf will be readily embraced, and will furnifh a frefh fupply of pleafures; fuch pleafures as are fecure from that wea-rinefs and difguft, which fooner or later are the confe-quences of all fuch enjoyments as tend merely to gra-tify the felfifh paffions and inclinations, and which always attend on an inactive ftate of mind, from whatever caufe it may proceed; whether it may be the effect of fatiety or difappointment, of profperity or defpair.

Even in the moft trifling fcenes of common life, the truly benevolent may find many pleafures, which would pafs unnoticed by others; and in a converfation, which to the thoughtlefs and inattentive would afford only a trifling amufement, or perhaps no amufement at all, they may find many fubjects for pleafing and ufeful reflections, which may conduce both to their happinefs and advantage; and that not only by being continually upon the watch for every opportunity of doing good to others, even in the moft trifling inftances, (which alone would afford a conftant fource of plea-fure) but alfo by the enjoyment of all the good they can obferve in others.

If

If any action is related, or any expreſſion dropped, which indicates true goodneſs of heart, they will be heard with ſatisfaction; the moſt trifling inſtance of kindneſs and attention will be received with a ſort of pleaſure of which the ſelfiſh can form no idea. Every appearance or deſcription of innocent happineſs will be enjoyed, every expreſſion of real friendſhip and affection will be felt, even though they are not the objects of it.

In ſhort, all the happineſs, and all the virtues of others, are ſources of delight to them; and it is a pleaſing, as well as uſeful exerciſe to the mind, to be employed, when engaged in ſociety, in ſeeking out for theſe;—to trace to their ſpring the little expreſſions of benevolence which often paſs unnoticed;—to diſcover real merit, through the veil which humility and modeſty throw over it;—to admire true greatneſs of mind, even in the meaneſt ſituation in life, or when it exerts itſelf upon occaſions ſuppoſed to be trifling, and therefore, in general, but little attended to.

In theſe and in numberleſs inſtances of the ſame kind, much real pleaſure might be found, which is too generally overlooked, and which might prove the ſource of many advantages, both to ourſelves and others; for thoſe who really enjoy the good of others, will certainly wiſh and endeavour to promote it. And by ſuch
exerciſes

exercifes as thefe, the beft affections of the heart are continually called forth to action, and the pleafures which they afford may be enjoyed and improved in every different fituation in life; for thefe are pleafures, which, more or lefs, are within the reach of all.

In thefe, the rich and profperous may find that fatisfaction which they have fought in vain in felfifh gratifications; and the afflicted may yet enjoy that happinefs which they are too apt to imagine is entirely loft:—but the felfifh heart can neither enjoy profperity, nor fupport affliction; it will be weary and diffatisfied in the firft, and totally dejected in the laft.

In order to adminifter confolation to the afflicted, the ufual methods are, either to endeavour to leffen their fenfe of the evil, by fhewing them that it is not really fo great as they imagine; or by comparing it with greater evils endured by others; or elfe to drive it from the thought by the hurry of diffipation and amufement.

The firft of thefe methods may ferve to difplay the talents of the perfon who undertakes it; and perhaps fuch arguments may fometimes prevail upon vanity to affume an appearance of fortitude. But how can he, whofe heart feels the pangs of real affliction, be convinced

vinced by argument that he does not feel it? or what
relief can it give to his fufferings, to be told that another fuffers more? Nor can diffipation and amufement
afford a more efficacious remedy, fince in thefe the
heart has nothing to do:—in the midft of the gayeft
fcenes, and furrounded by all that the world calls pleafure, it will fhrink into itfelf, and feel its own bitter-
nefs with redoubled force.

It is vain to endeavour to take from the wretched
the fenfe of fuffering; pain and grief muft be felt; they
can neither be fubdued by argument, nor loft in diffipation; and while they remain, it is impoffible to enjoy that eafe which by fome is reprefented as the
greateft good of man—they muft exclude it:—But
muft they therefore exclude all pofitive happinefs?
furely no. The wounded heart may ftill be open to
enjoyment, and here it muft feek for confolation; it
cannot indeed be infenfible of pain, but it may yet be
fenfible of pleafure. And happy indeed are they who
have acquired a relifh for fuch pleafures, as pain and
forrow cannot take away; fince thefe, fooner or later,
muft be the lot of all.

Of this kind are the pleafures of affection and benevolence; they enlarge the heart, they prevent it from
dwelling on its own forrows, and teach it to feek for
                                              happinefs

happinefs in the good of others; and thofe who in their happieft days were accuftomed to do this, will not become infenfible to fuch pleafures, becaufe they are themfelves in a ftate of fuffering.

Every inftance of kindnefs, every friendly endeavour to give eafe and comfort, will ftill rejoice the heart; the pleafure of feeing others virtuous and happy, may ftill be felt; the earneft defire to make them fo, may ftill be cherifhed; and that defire is in itfelf a pleafing fenfation. The endeavour which it excites affords ftill higher pleafure; and when that endeavour is bleffed with fuccefs, the benevolent heart will feel a real joy, to which its own fufferings cannot render it infenfible.

By every fuch exertion, the mind will gain new ftrength, and enjoy new pleafure; its native vigour, which forrow had depreffed, and which no interefted views could have called forth to action, will be reftored by benevolence;—the wounded heart may feel the delight of felf-approbation;—in fhort, the afflicted may enjoy the beft pleafures of the happy.

But after all it muft be allowed, that all our pleafures, in this imperfect ftate, even thofe of the moft refined and exalted kind, are liable to numberlefs forrows and difappointments. Friends may be removed by abfence,

or

or by death; the faults and imperfections of thofe we love, may wound the heart; affection may be repaid with unkindnefs, and benefits with ingratitude; the moft earneft endeavour to relieve the diftreffed, may prove unfuccefsful; and the fincereft defire to promote the happinefs of others, may mifs its aim: in fhort, every purfuit in this world may end in difappointment. And this thought might indeed be fufficient to check the ardour of the mind, and difcourage the beft endea-vours, had we not a never-failing refource in that affift-ance and fupport which Religion offers.

It is in the power of every one to fecure to himfelf a Happinefs of which nothing in this world can deprive him;—a Hope, which is not liable to difappointment; —a Friend, who never will forfake him, and who will be always willing and able to affift him.

Thofe who are placed in a happy fituation in this world, if at the fame time they can rejoice in fuch thoughts as thefe, may enjoy the good which they poffefs. Every blefling beftowed upon them will fill their hearts with love and gratitude to Him from whom it comes; and thefe fentiments will add new relifh to every pleafure, and make them become real and lafting advantages, means to promote their eternal felicity, not hindrances to ftop them in their way, as, by the perverfe ufe of them, they too often are.

Prompted by the fame love and gratitude, they will indeed rejoice in giving the beft proof of them, by an earneft endeavour to do good to others; and in this aim they cannot be difappointed, though they fhould prove unfuccefsful; for the honeft endeavour they may be certain will be accepted.

The fear of lofing the bleffings they poffefs, will not deprive them of the pleafure of enjoying them; for they remember in whofe hands they are; they know they fhall enjoy them as long as is really beft for them; and that if all elfe were taken from them, they are fe-cure of an unfailing refource, an Almighty Comforter.

They confider their beft enjoyments as independent on this world; the pleafures of friendfhip and benevo-lence, though here allayed by difappointment, and in-terrupted by death, they hope will be renewed hereafter, and enjoyed, pure and unmixed, through eternity.

The love and gratitude they feel, the delight they take in every means of expreffing them, will conftitute a part of their happinefs hereafter.

The heavenly contemplations which exalt their minds, and make them feel that they were formed for higher enjoyments than this world affords, will raife

G   their

their hopes to that ftate where alone they can find objects fuited to them.

And thus every blefling beftowed upon them will be fo received, that it will be truly enjoyed here, and will prove a fource of real and lafting happinefs: and the prefent good will neither be allayed by anxiety, nor fucceeded by wearinefs and difguft. While it remains, it will be enjoyed to the utmoft; and when it is taken away, it will not be immoderately regretted, fince that to which it owed its greateft relifh will ftill remain, and prove a fource of happinefs in the days of affliction and difappointment, as well as in thofe of profperity and fuccefs.

It is very certain that there are few, if any, either amongft the afflicted, or amongft the happy, who enjoy to the utmoft all the bleffings which are beftowed upon them. Thofe who take a view of their own fituation in life, with a fincere defire to make the beft of it, will probably find much more happinefs within their power, than in the moments of uneafinefs and difcontent they are apt to imagine. This obfervation is generally true, even of the greateft fufferers.

But let us fuppofe that this were not the cafe, for it muft be allowed to be poffible that all earthly comforts

forts may be taken away:—A perfon who has long been ftruggling againft the fevereft afflictions of body and of mind, may have met with nothing but difappointments; and in the midft of all, he may not find a friend to affift and fupport him, or to beftow that tender foothing confolation, which can almoft convert afflictions into pleafures; or, what is ftill more painful, the friend from whom he expected this may change, and embitter thofe fufferings he fhould alleviate; the endeavours to do good which benevolence infpires, may prove unfuccefsful; in a word, all in this world may fail.

This is indeed a cafe rarely, if ever, to be met with; but as it muft be allowed to be poffible, let us take things in the worft light imaginable, and then confider the happinefs which yet remains to balance thefe afflictions, in the heavenly comforts which religion offers.

The moft unhappy may yet find a Friend to whom they may freely unbofom all their forrows with the fulleft confidence, and reft fecure of finding that confolation which is really beft for them, fince He is both able and willing to beftow it:—this is a happinefs of which none but themfelves can ever deprive them. Though flighted and neglected, perhaps oppreffed and injured by the world, yet are they certain that He

G 2   regards

regards their fufferings, He hears their prayers, and will reward their patience.

When they confider that all events are at his difpofal, and thefe fufferings are permitted for their greater good, their fubmiffion, inftead of being full of terror and anxiety, will be an act of love and confidence;—even the wifh that they could choofe their own lot, will be fupprefled; and they will rejoice in the thought that Infinite Wifdom and Goodnefs will do it for them.

When they remember, that all afflictions are trials, and that by bearing them as they ought, they may beft exprefs their love and gratitude, and fecure his favour and protection,—the activity of their minds will be again awakened, and their utmoft efforts again exerted, with a pleafure and fatisfaction which can attend on no other purfuit, fince all but this are liable to difappointment. Here the intention, not the fuccefs, will be confidered: and the fincere wifh, when nothing more is in their power, will be accepted.

If we are engaged in the fervice of a friend, every difficulty becomes a fource of pleafure; we exert ourfelves with delight in finding means to conquer it; we even enjoy any fuffering which can procure his advantage, or exprefs our affection.

A fatis-

A fatisfaction of the fame kind may continually be enjoyed by the afflicted. It is true, their fufferings can bring no advantage to their Creator; his happinefs can receive no addition from the feeble efforts of his creatures; yet ftill, to a heart full of love and gratitude, there is a pleafure in exerting every effort to exprefs thofe fentiments, in doing or fuffering any thing which may conduce to that end. In this view, afflictions may be received with real fatisfaction, fince they afford continual opportunities of exprefling our readinefs to conform to his will, even when it is moft contrary to our own; and this is the ftrongeft proof of love and confidence we are able to give; and therefore, to the heart which truly feels them, muft be attended with a fatisfaction fuch as pleafure cannot beftow.

When we read the hiftories of thofe who have voluntarily undergone the moft painful fufferings, rather than tranfgrefs their duty, we admire their virtues, and efteem them happy. Thofe who receive as they ought the trials which are fent them, do all in their power to follow their examples, and may, in a great degree, enjoy the fame happinefs; their aims, their wifhes, are the fame; like them, they blefs him who permits the trial; they would deteft the thought of efcaping from it, by being guilty of the fmalleft crime: they rejoice in fuffering for his fake, and depend, with entire confidence, on his affiftance and fupport.   If

If at any time the affliction feems too fevere to be fupported, and nature almoft finks under the trial, let them anticipate the future time, and think with what fentiments they fhall look back upon it;—think, if they can, what joy it will afford them to reflect, that no fufferings could ever fhake their refolution; that their love to their Almighty Father, and defire to be conformable to his will, have been ftill the ruling principles of their hearts, even in the midft of the fevereft trials; that their afflictions have not made them neglect their duty to Him, or to their fellow-creatures; that their beft endeavours have been ftill exerted, and their entire confidence ever placed in Him.

Then let them look farther ftill, and think of the time when all earthly joys and forrows will be for ever paffed away, and nothing of them will remain but the manner in which they have been received; let them think of the happinefs of thofe who have been " made " perfect through fufferings," and who will then look forward to an eternity of blifs.

Will they then wifh that they had fuffered lefs? Or who would wifh it now, if fuch are the bleffed fruits of fufferings? And it depends on ourfelves to make them fo: for the affiftance of Him who alone can fupport our weaknefs, will never be wanting to thofe who feek it.

Such

Such reflections, such hopes, as thefe, can furely afford pleafures more than fufficient to overbalance any afflictions to which we may be liable in this world :— And *thefe* are pleafures which the greateft fufferer may feel, and in which the moft unhappy may rejoice.

To conclude:—Religion cannot prevent loffes and difappointments, pains and forrows; for to thefe, in this imperfect ftate, we muft be liable; nor does it require us to be infenfible to them, for that would be impoffible; but in the midft of all, and even when all earthly pleafures fail, it commands—it inftructs—it enables us to be happy.

CHARACTER OF LÆTITIA.

IN the midſt of a cheerful and animated converſation, the attention of a large company was ſuddenly called off by the tolling of a neighbouring bell, and the appearance of a funeral paſſing by the windows. An enquiry was made whoſe it was? with that ſort of indolent curioſity which is ſometimes excited by things ſuppoſed to be no way intereſting, and which hardly attends to the anſwer;—but a gloom was ſpread over every countenance, when it was known to be the funeral of the young and beautiful LÆTITIA, who had lately been the ornament of every aſſembly in which ſhe appeared, the admiration of all beholders, and the delight of all who knew her intimately.

As ſeveral in the company had been acquainted with LÆTITIA, the converſation naturally turned upon her character. The thought of youth and beauty thus nipped in their bloom, impreſſes an aweful yet tender melancholy in the minds even of indifferent

perſons,

perſons, which diſpoſes them to ſerious thoughts, and makes them anxious to know particulars; and the accounts now given of her engaged the attention of all who were preſent.

LÆTITIA had juſt entered her eighteenth year, her perſon was uncommonly beautiful, animated by all the vivacity which is natural to that age, and all the ſweet- neſs of the moſt amiable character.   Her youthful ſpi- rits had never been damped by ill health, nor checked by unkindneſs and ſeverity; her tender parents, far from reſtraining her pleaſures, had only endeavoured to ſecure them by innocence, improve them by virtue, and exalt them by religion.

The peace and joy of her heart diffuſed a charm on every object which ſurrounded her; and every employ- ment in which ſhe was engaged, afforded her new pleaſures;—ſhe purſued her ſtudies, and enjoyed her amuſements, with the ſame ſpirit and alacrity;—every kindneſs ſhe received filled her heart with gratitude, and all ſhe could beſtow was felt by her with that inno- cent exultation which true benevolence inſpires, and in which vanity claims no part.

In the fullneſs of her heart ſhe might have related ſome inſtance of diſtreſs which ſhe had relieved, with
the

the fame fentiments with which fhe related any other circumftance that afforded her the greateft pleafure; for it never entered her thoughts to admire herfelf for fuch things, or talk of them as if fhe was furprifed at herfelf for doing them. They appeared to her fo natural, that fhe imagined every one would have done the like, and only thought herfelf more fortunate than others, when an opportunity prefented itfelf for indulging her inclination.

From the fame principle proceeded her endeavours to pleafe in fociety. She wifhed to make all as happy as fhe could; fhe wifhed to deferve and gain affection; but fhe never thought of fupplanting others, or endeavouring to affume a fuperiority: and far from defiring to leffen their merits, in order to raife herfelf by the comparifon, fhe was eager to procure for all, the good which fhe valued herfelf, and therefore difpofed to reprefent all in the moft favourable light. Indeed, it coft her no difficulty to do fo, becaufe all appeared to her in that light. Happy in herfelf, and difpofed to be pleafed, her attention was naturally turned to the moft pleafing circumftances, in every event, and every character.

She often appeared delighted with things which others might have confidered as trifles, and that not
only

only in her amufements, but in the characters of thofe with whom fhe converfed. Her imagination was difpofed to magnify every good and amiable quality, and every little inftance of kindnefs and attention beftowed upon herfelf; but her affections, though warm and lively, were far from being indifcriminately lavifhed on all; her heart felt a kind word or look often much more ftrongly than it deferved, but its tendereft attachments were referved for a chofen few; and her friendfhip, like her benevolence, was ardent, animated, and difpofed to run almoft into excefs.

The fame difpofition appeared in other inftances. She enjoyed amufements as much as thofe who think of nothing but purfuing them, and even found pleafure where many would have thought they fhewed fuperior fenfe by being tired; but from the midft of the gayeft affembly, where her vivacity infpired pleafure to all around her, fhe would have flown at the call of benevolence, friendfhip, duty, or religion; and far from thinking fhe made a facrifice by doing fo, would have enjoyed the opportunity of exchanging a pleafure which only amufed her fancy, for one which touched her heart.

In common converfation, her innocent fprightlinefs, and artlefs fweetnefs of manners, won the hearts of
thofe

thofe who might have been inclined to envy her uncommon excellencies. There was a gentle earneftnefs
in her folicitude to pleafe, which animated every look
and action, and was far different from the ftudied difplay of vanity, and the artificial infinuations of flattery;
it fpoke her true and genuine fentiments, kept her continually upon the watch for every opportunity of expreffing her attention and regard for others, and added
a charm which can hardly be defcribed, even to the moft
trifling inftances of them.

The worft tempers were foftened in her prefence,
and the moft gloomy difpofitions could hardly avoid
fharing in her pleafures; yet the greateft flow of fpirits
could never, even for a fingle moment, make her lay
afide the gentlenefs and modefty of her character. She
even felt in a great degree, that timidity which is
natural to a delicate mind; but it ferved only to render
her converfation more engaging and interefting; it was
a diffidence of herfelf, not a fear of others.

In the midft of the moft playful fallies of her lively
fancy, and while fhe was gaining the admiration of all,
far from appearing to lay claim to it, her looks and
manners feemed continually to folicit their indulgence,
and fhewed that fhe thought fhe ftood in need of it;
yet accuftomed to encouragement from her infancy,

and

and judging of the benevolence of others by her own, she was difposed to feel a confidence in all, and to be very unguarded in her converfation; but the innocence of her heart afforded her a fecurity which the greateft caution cannot fupply;—she knew no difguife, but she had need of none.

She felt for the fufferings of others with the tendereft fenfibility, but she expreffed it, not by boafting of a fentiment which has no merit except in its application, but by an eagernefs to affift and relieve, which made her ready to attempt even impoffibilities; and by thofe gentle foothing attentions, from which even hopelefs diftrefs muft receive fome degree of pleafure. Her difpofition to enjoy every pleafure to the utmoft, made even the leaft fuccefs in her endeavours of this kind appear to her a happinefs which could hardly be too dearly purchafed.

Her early piety, far from allaying her pleafures, had added to every enjoyment the pleafing fentiment of love and gratitude to Him by whom they were beflowed, and the animating hope of brighter joys hereafter. She daily offered up the affections of her innocent heart to Him who made it, and implored his affiftance and protection, with that delightful confidence which true religion can alone infpire;—without this, her

her greateſt pleaſures would have wanted their higheſt
reliſh, and their beſt ſecurity; with it ſhe could enjoy
them without anxiety, and conſider them as the earneſt of future happineſs.

Such was LÆTITIA: when in the full bloom of
youth and health, which ſeemed to promiſe many
happy years, ſhe was ſeized with a ſudden illneſs,
which in a few days brought her to the grave.

An account like this could not fail to excite in the
mind of every hearer, reflections of the moſt ſerious
kind. Such ſtrokes as theſe, when youth, beauty,
and gaiety, are thus ſuddenly ſnatched away, are felt
even by the moſt thoughtleſs characters. The young
are warned to conſider the uncertainty of the advantages they poſſeſs, the vanity of every earthly pleaſure,
and the tranſient nature of thoſe qualities which are at
preſent the objects of general admiration; while thoſe
who are farther advanced in life, are taught ſtill more
powerfully the neceſſity of preparing for a change,
from which even youth and health are no ſecurity.

The importance of the preſent moment is impreſſed
on every mind, by the thought of the uncertainty of
the next. All acknowledge the folly of ſetting our
hearts on pleaſures juſt ready to eſcape from us, and
the

the neceffity of providing fuch comforts as may fupport us in that aweful hour which perhaps is now at
hand, and fuch hopes as death itfelf cannot take away.

Such are the reflections which naturally occur, when
a fudden ftroke brings home the thought of death to
every mind; efpecially when it has fallen where there
was leaft reafon to expect it, and when youth and beauty
render the object peculiarly interefting.

Such reflections afford an important and affecting
leffon, which all muft feel for the time, and of which
all fhould endeavour to preferve the impreffion.

In fuch a ftate of mind, when we confider religion
as our fupport and comfort in the hour of death, and
as affording us a happinefs which fhall laft beyond the
grave, all muft be fenfible of its value, and wifh to feel
its force, and obey its precepts, that they may fhare in
thofe bleflings which that religion can beftow.

But the thought of death, even when attended with
the moft ftriking circumftances, feldom makes a lafting
impreffion; and thofe who are merely awed into religion
by that confideration, may be too apt to lay it afide,
when a variety of other objects fucceed, and call off
their attention; or may connect the thought of it with
a gloomy

a gloomy idea, which difturbs their purfuits and their
enjoyments, and which therefore they are glad to drive
away. They feel themfelves well and happy; they
converfe with others who are fo; new fcenes arife, and
prefent objects make a ftrong impreffion; and in the
hurry of bufinefs or pleafure, the funeral of LÆTITIA
is quickly forgotten.

But it is not from her funeral alone that inftruction
may be derived. The thought of her early and unex-
pected death muft indeed imprefs an awe on every
mind, and lead to many reflections of the higheft importance to all; and which, by fuch a ftroke, are fhewn
in the ftrongeft and moft affecting light: but thofe
excited by her life and character may alfo afford many
ufeful leffons, which, though lefs obvious and ftriking,
are yet well worthy of our attention.

The pleafures of youth are often confidered, by thofe
who are farther advanced in life, with a mixture of
pity and contempt, as being the effects of ignorance of
the world, and of a kind of enthufiafm, which embellifhes every object, and feafts on imaginary enjoyments.
This opinion is certainly in fome degree true; for none
ever lived to maturity, without feeling and lamenting
the difappointment of their youthful hopes, and the lofs
of that pleafing illufion which once led the mind from

H   one

one enjoyment to another, and filled up the many tedious vacancies of real life; but the difappointment of too fanguine hopes is very apt to lead to a contrary extreme.

The pleafures of youth are indeed greatly owing to the difpofitions of the youthful mind; and thefe, it muft be owned, are often the effects of illufions, which time and experience muft difpel; but they are far from being always fo; and many of thofe difpofitions on which the pleafures of youth are founded, are fuch as the wife would wifh, and endeavour to preferve through every period of life.

That expectation of being pleafed, which prevails fo much in young perfons, is one great fource of their enjoyments. All are felt before hand, and their hopes are not eafily given up; the conviction that they fhall be pleafed, makes a ftrong impreffion on the imagination, which often lafts long enough to make them really be fo; when otherwife they would have found little reafon for it. This illufion cannot indeed be preferved in its full force, but the fame difpofition to be pleafed may yet remain; and there is hardly any thing of fo much importance to the happinefs of life.

We fee people feek for forrows, as if they were fomething very fcarce and valuable, which it would be a misfortune misfortnne to overlook. Would they but employ as much attention in feeking for the innocent pleafures which every different fituation might afford, and accuftom themfelves to coniider every thing in the moft favourable light, fuch a ftate of mind would in itfelf be pleafing, and would lead to many pleafures, which are too often loft merely for want of attending to them.

That defire to pleafe which is fo natural to youth, may indeed be difcouraged by difappointments, but if preferved through life, will prove a fource of pleafures to ourfelves and others. It can make even trifles appear agreeable and engaging, and will in a great degree fupply the want of every other talent, and render thofe who poffefs it always acceptable in fociety; often indeed much more fo than thofe who are far fuperior to them in every other refpect, but who neglect or defpife thofe little attentions which this difpofition will naturally infpire. Thefe fhould, however, always be diftinguifhed from artifice and flattery, which are the inftruments of vanity, not the expreffions of benevolence.

In youth, the affections of the heart are warm and lively; the pleafures, and even the hopes which they afford, are purfued, and enjoyed to the utmoft; probably they may lead to forrows and difappointments; but they know little of their own interefts, who endea-

vour

vour to avoid thefe, by checking that activity of the mind, which is neceffary to its improvement, as well as its happinefs; or by fuppreffing fentiments on which our enjoyments muft depend, and which (rightly directed) may prove the means of happinefs here and hereafter.

The innocence of youth is another great fource of its pleafures; but this is a happinefs, which, like that of health, is generally eftimated by its lofs.

It is not neceffary to confider the fituation of a perfon who has been guilty. of great crimes; all muft be enfible that it is wretched; but many things, which, taken feparately, may appear trifles, are yet fufficient to deftroy that purity of heart without which every pleafure muft be attended with fome allay. This indeed, in the ftricteft fenfe of the words, is not to be found in this imperfect ftate, even in youth itfelf; ftill lefs can it be expected in thofe who are farther advanced in life.

But innocence of intention, integrity of heart, and a fincere endeavour to do right, are qualities which all may poffefs, and which afford a fecurity and peace of mind, fuch as they can never enjoy who are in any degree wanting in them; whofe profeffions differ from their fentiments; and who indulge themfelves in thofe
little

little arts which vanity or self-intereſt ſo often ſuggeſt, and which are ſo common in the general intercourſe of ſociety, that the particular inſtances of them are ſeldom made the objects of attention, or conſidered in the light of real faults.

The candour of mind, and unſuſpecting temper, ſo natural to youth, are alſo productive of many pleaſures which painful experience muſt in ſome degree deſtroy. But how many, by the thought of this, are led into errors far more pernicious, and often not leſs diſtant from the truth; for ſuſpicion can deceive, as well as ſimplicity, and frequently miſſes the mark as effectually, by going beyond it.

How greatly is the peace of ſociety diſturbed, by offences taken which never were intended, by groundleſs doubts and apprehenſions, and by the imputation of faults and bad intentions which never in reality exiſted!

To avoid all error is certainly deſirable, but the one extreme is liable to it, as well as the other; and that diſpoſition of mind, which in caſes that can admit a doubt inclines rather to the moſt favourable ſide, is certainly by far the happieſt for the poſſeſſor, to ſay nothing of the obligations which benevolence and charity lay upon us in this reſpect.

H 3 Such

Such reflections as thefe may naturally arife from
the confideration of a character like that of LÆTITIA.
Her youth affords many ufeful leffons to grey hairs,
as well as to thofe who like herfelf are juft entering
into life, and who perhaps, like her, may be allowed
only a few fhort years to prepare themfelves for eternity.
Her death fets in a ftrong light the neceffity of fuch
preparation;—her life fhews at the fame time the happinefs of it.

That Religion is neceffary to our comfort in the
time of affliction, and our fupport in the hour of death,
all who have any fenfe of it are ready to allow; but if
confidered merely in that light, it is too apt to be neglected in the days of health and profperity, or obeyed
with a cold, and often reluctant fubmiffion, as a reftraint with which it is neceffary to comply, in order
to obtain the happinefs of a future ftate. Few confider
fufficiently its importance to happinefs, even in this life,
and the prefent pleafures, as well as future hopes,
which it may afford to thofe in whom it is not merely
a conviction of the underftanding, but a real fentiment
of the heart.

Let us then reprefent to ourfelves the fituation of
thofe on whom the great truths which Religion reveals
have made a juft impreffion; who feel that love and
gratitude

gratitude which are due to Infinite Perfection and Infinite Goodnefs; and in whom thefe fentiments are the leading principles and animating motives for every action.

To fuch perfons, how delightful is the thought, that they are under the guidance and protection of an indulgent Father, who can and will order all things for their real good; that every blefling beftowed in this life is not merely a prefent enjoyment, but an inftance of his goodnefs, a call to that ever-pleafing fentiment —affectionate gratitude, and an earneft of future happinefs! Such thoughts give a fecurity to all pleafures; they are no longer enjoyed with trembling anxiety, from a dread that the next moment may fnatch them away; for the next moment depends on an Almighty Friend, with whom we can fafely intruft our deareft interefts.

It has been well obferved, by an excellent writer, *Qu'il n'y a point de fentiment plus doux au cœur de l'homme que la confiance*; but if this be true, even in our intercourfe with frail and imperfect beings, in whom we may be miftaken; and who, though their intentions may be fincerely good, are often unable to help us, and ignorant of what is beft for us; how much greater enjoyment muft it afford, when fixed where it can

never

never be miftaken or difappointed! How encouraging is the certainty, that He, who fees the deepeft receffes of the heart, will obferve and accept the fecret good intention which could not be brought to effect, and the fincere endeavour which has been difappointed, and perhaps mifinterpreted in this world.

To relieve diftrefs, to do good to others and promote their happinefs, muft give pleafure to every one who is not loft to all fenfe of goodnefs; but how greatly is this pleafure increafed, if the object on whom it is exercifed be endeared to us by particular affection, or has been recommended to us by one who is fo, and to whom we can in this manner exprefs our affection! What fpirit does this confideration give to our endeavours, and what an exalted pleafure attends their fuccefs!

This pleafure, in the higheft degree, Religion adds to every exertion of benevolence. It ftrengthens the ties of natural philanthropy, by fhewing us in all mankind the children of one Common Parent, the objects of the fame Redeeming Love, and the candidates for the fame Eternal Happinefs. In every fcene of diftrefs to which we can afford relief, it reminds us, that our beft Friend has affured us, that whatever is done to one of the leaft of thefe his brethren, will be confidered as done unto himfelf: and this pleafure
depends

depends not on fuccefs; for the endeavour, and even the *wifh*, will be accepted as a proof of love and gratitude.

From the fame confideration, Religion becomes the only fure foundation of that good-humour which is the charm of focial life.   Can beings, who hope in a few years, perhaps in a few hours, to be united in eternal love and happinefs, be difpofed to be angry with each other about trifles, and find a fatisfaction in faying or doing what may give pain?

Were thefe truths felt as well as acknowledged, they muft not only put an end to all violent hatred and animofity, but muft alfo foften all thofe little irregularities of temper, which fo frequently prevent even good people from being as happy in each other as they ought to be.

At the fame time, when we are hurt by fuch things in others, particularly in thofe we truly love and value, (and from whom, therefore, a trifle can give pain) how pleafing to look forward to the time when all thefe imperfections fhall be ended, and we fhall find nothing to allay the pleafures of affection and efteem; which in this life can never be enjoyed in their utmoft perfection, from the mixture of human frailty which is found in a greater or lefs degree even in truly worthy characters.   But

But when friendſhip riſes to its pureſt heights, and meets with as little of ſuch allay as is poſſible in this imperfect ſtate, ſtill how greatly are even the refined pleaſures which it affords improved and exalted by Religion! How delightful is the tie which unites two worthy characters in the nobleſt purſuits, when each is ſtrengthened and animated by the other; and their pleaſures, far from being allayed by the continual dread of ſeparation, are heightened by the hope that they will be laſting as eternity!

When the mind is engaged in the purſuit of improvement, and pleaſed with any little advance it can make; or when it delights itſelf with the conſideration of what is beautiful and amiable in the natural or moral ſyſtem; how greatly is the pleaſure increaſed by looking forward to a time, when every faculty ſhall be improved beyond what we can at preſent conceive, when we ſhall be qualified for the moſt exalted enjoyments, and all our contemplations employed in the moſt perfect objects!——But when we endeavour to enlarge on a ſubject like this, we muſt find all our expreſſions fall ſhort of what we wiſh to deſcribe.

Theſe are but a few inſtances of the advantages which may be derived from Religion, even in the happieſt ſtate,—a faint ſketch of its power to refine, exalt,

and

and fecure our pleafures.   Happy they to whom experience fhall give a more perfect idea of it!   They will
not be reduced, in the day of affliction, to feek for comforts with which they were before unacquainted, and
pleafures which they know not how to enjoy; for the
beft pleafures of their happieft days will remain, unal-
layed by any misfortune that can befall them; and the
mind, long accuftomed to dwell on them and enjoy
them, will grow more attached to them, as other pleafures fail, and be enabled to look forward to the ftroke
which fhall fnatch them all away, not only with calm
refignation, but with joyful hope.

Far be it ever from us to limit the mercies of the
Almighty, or difcourage any from having recourfe to
them, even in their lateft moments.   Far be it alfo
from us to judge of the future happinefs of any, by their
prefent ftate of mind.   An old age of languor and
dejection, a death of terror and anxiety, may often be
fucceeded by an eternity of blifs.

But let thofe who now enjoy health and profperity never forget, that they can have no reafon to depend on finding Religion their comfort in the hour
of death, if they do not find it their happinefs in life.

POLITENESS.

———

" L'HYPOCRISIE eſt un hommage que le vice
" rend à la vertu," ſays LA ROCHEFOUCAULT; and
in one ſenſe it certainly is ſo, for it is an acknowledge-
ment of the ſuperior excellence of virtue; and one
who viewed mankind with the eyes of LA ROCHE-
FOUCAULT, muſt conſider Hypocriſy as an advantage
to all.

ROUSSEAU, quoting this paſſage, adds, " Oui
" comme celui des aſſaſſins de Ceſar, qui ſe proſter-
" noient à ſes pieds pour l'egorger plus ſurement;
" couvrir ſa mechanceté du dangereux manteau de
" l'Hypocriſie, ce n'eſt point honorer la Vertu, c'eſt
" l'outrager en profanant ſes enſeignes." It is indeed
the homage of an enemy; and of all the enemies of
virtue, there is perhaps none whoſe attacks have been
more pernicious; and that not only by throwing a
diſguiſe over vice, but by ſetting up an artificial image
in the place of real virtue, and confounding the idea
of

of the one with the other, till every appearance is fuf-
pe&ed, and the exiftence of that which is true and
genuine is rendered doubtful, to thofe whofe hearts do
not bear teftimony to its certainty.

There is hardly any thing which (confidered abftrac-
tedly) appears fo natural as Sincerity.   Speech was
given us to exprefs our thoughts and feelings; and to
ufe it to exprefs what we do not think and feel, is an
evident perverfion of it.   But alas! man, fallen from
his native innocence, now *dares* not be fincere; confcious of guilt, he feeks difguife; and confcious of difguife
in himfelf, he is ready to fufpe& it in others.

Thus infincerity firft made its way amongft mankind, and by fuch confiderations it has fince been cherifhed and encouraged, though every heart in fecret
bears teftimony againft it; and even amongft the greateft
hypocrites, few would venture openly to defend it in
matters of importance: in thefe all are ready to declare
againft it, and fincerity is a quality to which all lay claim;
yet in the daily occurrences of common life, it feems
to be laid afide by a kind of tacit agreement: few make
any fcruple of deviating from it themfelves, or feem to
expe& a conformity to it in others: but deceit is practifed when it can anfwer any purpofe, and even acknowledged on many occafions, as if it were in itfelf a
matter of the greateft indifference.   It

It is much too common, in every inftance, to judge of actions, not according to what they really are, but according to the impreffion they make upon us. The man who would be fhocked at the thought of being a butcher, will feel no remorfe at impaling a butterfly; and he who would fcorn to tell a folemn lie, will make no fcruple of profeffing efteem and regard which he does not feel, or of encouraging an unexperienced young woman in follies which in his heart he defpifes, and which he knows will render her ridiculous. Yet the merit of actions depends not on their apparent ef-fects, nor are we fufficiently acquainted with the con-fequences which may attend them, to be qualified to judge how far they may extend.

When once we deviate from the ftraight path, how-ever fmall the deviation may be, and however ftrong the reafons for it, we can never know how far we may be led aftray, nor what may be the confequences of that deviation. Could thefe be known at once, the fault which was confidered merely as a trifle, would often appear fhocking, even to thofe who paid leaft attention to it, though in fact they can make no differ-ence in its real nature.

If infincerity be in itfelf a fault, it muft be fo inde-pendent of the confequences which may follow from it;

it; yet the moſt trifling conſideration ſeems often to be thought a ſufficient excuſe for it, and we even hear it pleaded for, as neceſſary to the peace and pleaſure of ſociety. But to whom can it be neceſſary? Surely to none but thoſe who have ſomething criminal, or at leaſt ſomething diſagreeable, to conceal, and whoſe real characters will not bear the light. The good and amiable qualities want only to be ſeen as they are, in order to be pleaſing and uſeful; and if every heart were ſuch as it ought to be, the delight of ſociety would be to throw aſide all diſguiſe, let every one expreſs his genuine ſentiments, and appear to others ſuch as he really is.

But it is eaſier to poliſh the manners, than to reform the heart; to diſguiſe a fault, than to conquer it. He who can venture to appear as he is, muſt be what he ought to be;—a difficult and arduous taſk! which often requires the ſacrifice of many a darling inclination, and the exertion of many a painful effort:—and if there can be any hope of attaining the ſame end by a ſhorter and eaſier method, it is not wonderful that numbers are glad to have recourſe to it.

This is, in fact, the principal cauſe of that inſincerity which prevails ſo much in the ordinary intercourſe of ſociety, though there are many others which contribute to it.

Pride

Pride makes men endeavour to feem better than they really are, by affuming an appearance of thofe virtues which they want, and endeavouring to difguife thofe vices which they cherifh.

Selfifhnefs makes them wifh to engrofs a larger fhare of efteem and regard than is beftowed on others; this introduces flattery, which is, in fact, an endeavour to purchafe efteem, and even affection, with counterfeit coin. It is playing upon the weakneffes of others for our own advantage, and running the hazard of encouraging them in folly, and even in vice; and thereby doing them a real and material injury, merely for the fake of gaining to ourfelves the trifling fatisfaction of unmerited approbation.

This, to a perfon of any delicacy, fhould give more pain than pleafure, from a confcioufnefs of having indeed deferved the contrary: for who, that is not loft to every generous fentiment, could bear to receive a tribute of gratitude and good-will, in return for profeffions of efteem which he never felt, and kindnefs which he never intended? He may indeed defpife the folly and vanity of thofe who can be pleafed with fuch profeffions, and poffibly they may often be deferving of contempt; but this is no alleviation of his fault, nor can even this excufe be always pleaded.

I   An

An innocent heart may be pleafed with the flattery (without giving entire credit to it) when it is confidered as an expreffion of real kindnefs: confcious that its own fentiments are warm, lively, and apt to run into excefs, it may naturally fuppofe the fame of others; and thus the poifon is received under a pleafing difguife, till by degrees it grows familiar, and may produce the moft fatal effects.

True Politenefs—like true Benevolence, the fource from which it flows—aims at the real good of all mankind, and fincerely endeavours to make all eafy and happy, not only by confiderable fervices, but by all thofe little attentions which can contribute to it. In this it differs effentially from that artificial politenefs which too often affumes its place, and which confifts in an endeavour, not to make others happy, but to ferve the interefts of our own vanity, by gaining their favour and good opinion, though at the expence of truth, goodnefs, and even of their happinefs, if the point in view can be obtained by deftroying it.

Flattery is an effential part of this fort of politenefs, the means by which it generally fucceeds: but true politenefs ftands in need of no fuch affiftance; it is the genuine expreffion of the heart, it feeks no difguife, and will never flatter. He who acts from this principle,

ciple, will exprefs to all what he truly feels,—a real good-will, a fincere concern for their happinefs, and an earneft defire to promote it. He will not exprefs admiration for a fool, nor efteem for a bad man; but he will exprefs benevolence to all, becaufe he feels it; and he will endeavour to do them good, as far as may be in his power, becaufe he fincerely wifhes it.

Flattery is directly contrary to this; it feeks its own ends, without confidering what may be the confequence with regard to others. It is alfo effentially different from that regard which is paid to real merit; for that is a tribute which is certainly its due, and may be both paid and received with innocence and pleafure: but the expreffions of this will generally be fuch as efcape undefignedly from the heart, and are far different from the ftudied language of flattery.

Indeed flattery is not, in general, addreffed to real and acknowledged merit. It has been obferved by one who feems to have ftudied it as a fcience, that a profeffed beauty muft not be complimented upon her perfon, but her underftanding, becaufe there fhe may be fuppofed to be more doubtful of her excellence; while one whofe pretenfions to beauty are but fmall, will be moft flattered by compliments on her perfonal charms.

The

The fame may be obferved as to other qualities: for though moft people would confider flattery as an infult, if addreffed to fuch qualities as they know they do not poffefs; yet in general they are beft pleafed with it where they feel any degree of doubt, or fufpect that others may do fo.

When Cardinal RICHELIEU expreffed more defire to be admired as a poet and a critic, than as one of the greateft politicians in the world, we cannot fuppofe it was becaufe he thought thefe talents of more confequence in a prime minifter; but he was certain of his excellence in one refpect, and wanted not to be told what all the world muft think of him; in the other he wifhed to excel, and was not fure of fuccefs.

The fame may probably be the reafon of the partiality which fome writers are faid to have expreffed for their worft performances. It feems fcarcely poffible to fuppofe that MILTON really preferred his Paradife Regained to his Paradife Loft; but if he had any doubts of its fuccefs, it was very natural for him to feel more anxiety about it, and to endeavour to perfuade others, and even himfelf, of its fuperior merit.

This is a weaknefs in human nature, of which flattery generally takes advantage, without confidering,
that

that by fuch means it not only encourages vanity in
thofe to whom it is addreffed, but may alfo draw them
in, to make themfelves appear ridiculous, by the affectation of qualities to which they have little or no pretenfions.

Nor does this artificial kind of flattery generally ftop
at fuch qualities as are in themfelves indifferent; it is
too often employed (and perhaps ftill more fuccefsfully)
in difguifing and palliating faults, and thereby affording
encouragement to thofe whofe inclinations were reftrained by fome degree of remorfe.

It is unjuft as well as ill-natured, to take advantage
of the weakneffes of others, in order to obtain our
own ends, at the hazard of rendering them ridiculous;
but it is fomething far worfe to lend a helping hand to
thofe who hefitate at engaging in the paths of vice,
and feel a painful confli&t between their duty and their
inclination; or to endeavour to leffen the fenfe of duty
in thofe who are not free from fome degree of remorfe,
and defire to amend. Yet thefe are, in general, the
perfons to whom flattery is moft acceptable:—it
foothes their inclinations, and difpels their doubts, at
the fame time that it gratifies their vanity; it frees
them from a painful fenfation, and faves them the
trouble of a difficult tafk, while it affords them a pre-

I 3   fent

fent pleafure; and if it does not entirely conquer their
fcruples, at leaſt it removes one reſtraint which lay in
their way, the fear of being cenfured. Yet how often
is all this done by thofe who would think themfelves
infufferably injured, if they were to be fuppofed capable
of picking a pocket, though in that cafe the injury
might perhaps be trifling, and hardly worth a thought.

If " he who filches from me my good name," has
made me " poor indeed;" what ſhall we fay of him,
who from felfiſh views, perhaps merely for the fake of
obtaining a trifling gratification of his vanity, has done
what may lead me to deferve to forfeit that good name,
even in the fmalleſt inſtance? And if he has done this
by deceit, and has found means to gain affection or
eſteem in return for it, what other act of diſhoneſty
can exceed·the bafenefs of fuch proceeding? But thefe
things are too apt to make little impreſſion when practifed in what are called trifles, though that circum-
ſtance makes no change in their real nature, and none
can fay how far the confequences even of trifles may
extend.

Thofe who make no fcruple of fuch methods as
thefe, if at the fame time, by being much accuſtomed
to polite company, they have acquired a certain ele-
gance of manners, and facility of expreffing themfelves,
                                                will

will feldom fail to pleafe, upon a flight acquaintance; but the beft actor will find it difficult always to keep up to his part.

He who is polite only by rule, will probably, on fome occafion or other, be thrown off his guard; and he who is continually profeffing fentiments which he does not feel, will hardly be able always to do it in fuch a manner as to avoid betraying himfelf.

Whatever degree of affection or efteem is gained without being deferved, though at firft it may be both paid and received with pleafure, will probably, after a time, vanifh into nothing, or prove a fource of difappointment and mortification to both parties; and, even while the delufion lafts, it is fcarce poffible it fhould be attended with entire fatisfaction to the deceiver; for deceit of all kinds, from the greateft to the moft trifling inftance of it, muft be attended with a degree of anxiety, and can never enjoy that perfect eafe and fecurity, which attends on thofe whofe words and actions are the natural undifguifed expreffions of the fentiments of the heart.

But as mankind are apt to run from one extreme to another, we fometimes fee, that from a diflike to this artificial politenefs, which is continually gloffing

over

over faults, both in thofe who practife it, and thofe they practife it upon, a roughnefs and even brutality of manners is adopted, and dignified with the title of fincerity.

Some perfons pique themfelves upon faying all they think, and are continually profeffing to do fo; and as a proof of this, they will fay things the moft fhocking to others, and give them pain without the leaft remorfe, for fear of being fufpected of flattering them. But is this then the language of their heart? Alas! if it be fo, let them fet about reforming it, and make it fit to be feen, before they make their boaft of expofing it to public view: yet perhaps there may be as much affectation in this conduct as in the contrary extreme.

Pride may think to gain its own ends by an appearance of fingularity, and by fetting itfelf above the approbation of others, as vanity does by condefcending to the meaneft methods, in order to obtain it.

That fincerity which is difplayed with oftentation, is generally to be fufpected. The conduct which an honeft heart infpires flows naturally from it; and thofe who fay rough things, in order to convince others of their fincerity, give fome reafon to doubt of their being perfectly convinced of it themfelves.

Both

Both thefe extremes are not only pernicious to the prefent peace and pleafure of fociety, but may alfo lead to very fatal confequences.

The flatterer encourages vice and folly, undermines the principles of virtue, and gains, by fraud and artifice, a degree of efteem and regard to which he has no title. The other does what he can to frighten every one from what is right; for if finceriy difcover fuch a heart, dif- guife muft appear defirable; and few confider fufficiently how much the caufe of virtue muft fuffer, whenever a good quality is made to appear in an unamiable light.

Sincerity is indeed the ground-work of all that is good and valuable; however beautiful in appearance the ftructure may be, if it ftand not on this foundation, it cannot laft. But fincerity can hardly be called a virtue in itfelf, though a deviation from it is a fault:— A man may be fincere in his vices, as well as in his virtues; and he who throws off all reftraint of remorfe or fhame, and even makes a boaft of his vices, can claim no merit from the fincerity he expreffes in fo doing.

If he who is *fincere* cannot appear *amiable*, his heart is wrong, and his fincerity, far from being a virtue, ferves only to add to the reft of his faults that of being
willing

willing to give pain to others, and able to throw afide
that fhame which fhould attend on every fault, whether great or fmall, and which is fometimes a reftraint
to fuch as are incapable of being influenced by nobler
motives.

Roughnefs of manners is in fact fo far from being
in itfelf a mark of finccrity, that it is merely the natural
expreffion of *one* character, as gentlenefs is of *another*;
and it fhould always be remembered, that to connect
the idea of a good quality with a difagreeable appearance, is doing it a real **injury**, and leads to much more
pernicious confequences than may at firft be apprehended.   Yet this is too often done, in many inftances,
not only by thofe who are interefted to promote fuch
a deception, but alfo by thofe who take up maxims
upon credit, and believe what others have believed,
without enquiring into the grounds of fuch opinions:
and this is too much the cafe with the world in general.

Much has been faid and written on the fubject of
Politenefs; but thofe who attempt to teach it, generally
begin where they fhould end; and the inftruction they
give is fomething like teaching a fet of elegant phrafes
in a language not underftood, or inftructing a perfon
in mufic, by making him learn a few tunes by memory, without any knowledge of the grounds of the
science.

fcience. The polifh of elegant manners is indeed truly
pleafing, and neceffary in order to make the worthieft
character compleatly amiable; but it fhould be a *polifh*,
and not a *varnifh*; the ornament of a good heart, not
the difguife of a bad one.

Where a truly benevolent heart is joined with a delicate mind, and both are directed by a folid and refined underftanding, the natural expreffion of thefe
qualities will be the effential part of true politenefs.
All the reft is mere arbitrary cuftom, which varies according to the manners of different nations, and different times. A conformity to this is, however, highly
neceffary; and thofe who neglect to acquire the knowledge and practice of it, betray the want of fome of the
above-mentioned qualities.

A perfon might as well refufe to fpeak the language
of a country, as to comply with its cuftoms in matters
of indifference; like it, they are figns which, though
unmeaning perhaps in themfelves, are eftablifhed by
general confent to exprefs certain fentiments; and a
want of attention to them would appear to exprefs a
want of thofe fentiments, and therefore, in regard to
others, would have the fame bad effect. But though
the neglect of thefe things be blameable, thofe who
confider them as the effential part of true politenefs are
much

much wider of the mark, for they may be ſtrictly obſerved where that is entirely wanting.

To wound the heart, to miſlead the underſtanding, to diſcourage a timid character, to expoſe an ignorant, though perhaps an innocent one, with numberleſs other inſtances in which a real injury is done, are things by no means inconſiſtent with the *rules* of politeneſs, and are often done by ſuch as would not go out of the room before the perſon they have been treating in this manner; for though doing ſuch things openly might be conſidered as ill-manners, there are many indirect ways which are juſt as effectual, and which may be practiſed without any breach of eſtabliſhed forms. Like the Phariſees of old, they are ſcrupulous obſervers of the letter of the law in trifles, while they neglect the ſpirit of it: and their obſervance of forms, far from giving any reaſon to depend on them, on the contrary often ſerves them only as a ſhelter, under which they can do ſuch things as others would not dare to venture upon.

This is alſo, in general, only put on (like their beſt dreſs) when they are to go into company; for whenever politeneſs is not the natural expreſſion of the heart, it muſt be in ſome degree a reſtraint, and will therefore probably be laid aſide in every unguarded
hour,

hour, that is to fay, in all their intercourfe with thofe whom it is of moft confequence to them to endeavour to make happy:—And the unhappinefs which fome-times reigns in families, who really poffefs many good qualities, and are not wanting in mutual affection, is often entirely owing to a want of that true and fincere politenefs which fhould animate the whole conduct, though the manner of expreffing it muft be different according to different circumftances.

Politenefs is always neceffary to compleat the happi-nefs of fociety in every fituation, from the accidental meeting of ftrangers, to the moft intimate connections of families and friends; but it muft be the genuine ex-preffion of the fettled character, or it cannot be con-ftant and univerfal.

Let us then endeavour to confider the true founda-tion of that ever-pleafing quality diftinguifhed by the name of Politenefs, leaving the ornamental part of it, like other ornaments, to be determined by the fafhion of the place and time.

To enter fully into the detail of fuch a character, would be an arduous tafk indeed; but the flighteft fketch of what is truly pleafing cannot fail to afford fome fatisfaction; and there can hardly be a more ufeful

ful exercife to the mind, than to dwell on the confideration of good and amiable qualities, to endeavour to improve upon every hint, and raife our ideas of excellence as high as poffible. We may then apply them to our own conduct in the ordinary occurrences of life; we may obferve in what inftances we fall fhort of that perfection we wifh to attain, endeavour to trace the caufe of the want of it in thofe inftances, and learn not to difguife our faults, but to amend them.

True benevolence infpires a fincere defire to promote the happinefs of others:—True delicacy enables us to enter into their feelings; it has a quick fenfe of what may give pleafure or pain, and teaches us to purfue the one, and avoid the other:—And a refined underftanding points out the fureft means of doing this in different circumftances, and of fuiting our conduct to the perfons with whom we are concerned. The union of all thefe will conftitute that amiable character, of which true politenefs is the genuine and natural expreffion.

The perfon who has not thefe qualities may indeed, by other means, attain to fomething like politenefs on fome occafions; but the perfon who poffeffes them in perfection, can never be wanting in it, even for a moment, in any inftance, or in any company;—with fuperiors

riors and inferiors, with ftrangers and with friends, the
fame character is ftill preferved, though expreffed in
different ways. Thofe pleafing attentions, which are
the charm of fociety, are continually paid with eafe
and fatisfaction, for they are the natural language of
fuch fentiments; and to fuch a character it would be
painful to omit them; while every thing that can give
unneceffary pain, even in the fmalleft degree, is conftantly avoided, becaufe directly contrary to it; for no
pain can be inflicted by a perfon of fuch a difpofition,
without being ftrongly felt at the fame time.

A fuperior degree of delicacy may often be the caufe
of much pain to thofe who poffefs it; they will be hurt
at many things which would make no impreffion upon
others; but from that very circumftance, they will be
taught to avoid giving pain on numberlefs occafions,
when others might do it. Whenever an excefs of
fenfibility is fuppofed to produce a contrary effect, we
may be certain it is, in fact, an excefs of felfifhnefs.

True delicacy feels the pain it receives, but it feels
much more ftrongly the pain it gives; and therefore
will never give any, which it is poffible to avoid. Far
from being the caufe of unreafonable complaints, uneafinefs, and fretfulnefs, it will always carefully avoid
fuch things; it will know how to make allowances for
others,

others, and rather fuffer in filence, than give them unneceffary pain. It will infpire the gentleft and moft
engaging methods of helping others to amend their
faults, and to correct thofe irregularities of temper
which difturb the peace of fociety, without expofing
them to the humiliation of being upbraided, or even
of being made fully fenfible of the offence they give;
which often difpofes people rather to feek for excufes,
than to endeavour to amend. In fhort, it enlightens
and directs benevolence; difcovers numberlefs occafions for the exertion of it, which are too generally
overlooked; and points out the fureft and moft pleafing
means of attaining thofe ends which it purfues.

This earneft defire to promote the happinefs of all,
which is effential to true politenefs, fhould always be
carefully diftinguifhed from that defire of pleafing, in
which felf-love is in fact the object; for though this
may fometimes appear to produce the fame effects with
the other, it is by no means fufficient fully to fupply its
place. It is indeed a natural fentiment, which is both
pleafing and ufeful when kept within due bounds.

To gain the good-will of others, is foothing to the
heart; and they muft be proud or infenfible, in a very
uncommon degree, who are not defirous of it: but
much more than this is neceffary to infpire true and
                                        conftant

conftant politenefs in every inftance; and this defire, carried to excefs, may produce very pernicious confequences.

From hence fometimes proceed endeavours to fupplant others in the favour of thofe we wifh to pleafe, and to recommend ourfelves at their expence, together with all the train of evils which attend on envy and jealoufy.

From hence alfo flattery, and all thofe means of gaining favour, by which the real good of others is facrificed to our own intereft; and from hence much of the infincerity which prevails in common converfation. Falfe maxims are adopted, and the real fentiments difguifed; a difpofition to ridicule, cenforioufnefs, and many other faults, are encouraged; and truth and goodnefs are facrificed to the fear of giving offence: and thus an inclination in itfelf innocent, and calculated to promote the pleafure and advantage of fociety, is made productive of much evil, by being fuffered to act beyond its proper fphere, and to take place of others which fhould always be preferred before it.

But even confidered in the moft favourable light, the defire of pleafing others falls far fhort of that endeavour to make them happy which benevolence infpires;

K   for

for the one is only exerted in fuch inftances as can gain obfervation; the other extends to every thing within its power, and can facrifice even the defire of pleafing, to that of doing real good, whenever the one is inconfiftent with the other.   Yet where this is done with that true politenefs which is the effect of thofe qualities already mentioned, it is very likely to fucceed better in the end, even as to gaining favour with all thofe whofe favour is truly valuable: but it depends not on fuch circumftances; it is a fettled character, which is naturally difplayed in every inftance, without art or ftudy.

It may alfo be obferved, that though a great degree of affection may fubfift where this quality is wanting, yet that want will always prove an allay to the pleafure of it.

We fee perfons who really feel this affection, who would do and fuffer a great deal to ferve each other, and would confider a feparation by abfence or death as one of the greateft of evils; and who yet, merely from the want of this quality, lofe a thoufand opportunities of promoting the happinefs of thofe they truly love and value, and often give them real pain, without ever fufpecting themfelves of being wanting in regard and affection, becaufe they feel that they would be ready to exert themfelves in doing them any effential fervice.

Thus

Thus the pleasure of society is deftroyed, and the fuppofed confcioufnefs of poffeffing good qualities (for the exertion of which it is poffible no opportunity may ever offer) is thought to make amends for the want of fuch as are truly pleafing and ufeful in every day and hour of our intercourfe with each other.

Happinefs confifts not in fome extraordinary inftance of good fortune, nor virtue in fome illuftrious exertion of it; for fuch things are in the power of few: but if they are true and genuine, the one muft be practifed, and the other enjoyed, in the conftant and uniform tenor of our lives.

The perfon who on fome extraordinary occafions does another fome fignal piece of fervice, is by no means fo great a benefactor, as one who makes his life eafy and happy by thofe pleafing attentions, the fingle inftances of which too often pafs unnoticed, but which altogether form the delight of focial intercourfe, and afford a calm and ferene pleafure, without which, the moft profperous fortune can never beftow happinefs.

There is a fecurity in all our intercourfe with per-fons of this character, which banifhes that continual anxiety, and dread of giving offence, which fo often throw a reftraint on the freedom of converfation.

K 2   Such

Such perfons wifh all mankind to be amiable and happy, and therefore would certainly do their utmoft to make them fo; and far from taking offence where none was intended, they will be difpofed to fee all in the moft favourable light; and even where they cannot approve, they will never be fevere in their cenfures on any, but always ready to endeavour to bring them back to what is right, with that gentlenefs and delicacy, which fhew it is for their fakes they wifh it, and not in refentment of an injury received, or with a view to affume to themfelves a fuperiority over them.

They will make allowances for all the little peculiarities of humour, all the weakneffes, and even the faults as far as poffible, of thofe with whom they converfe, and carefully avoid whatever may tend to irritate and aggravate them; which is often done by fuch things as would be trifling and indifferent in other circumftances. This not only has a bad effect, by giving prefent uneafinefs, but ferves to ftrengthen a bad habit; for every fault (particularly a fault of the temper) is increafed by exercife; and trifles, which might have been immediately forgotten, are kept up by being taken notice of, till they become real evils.

They will alfo carefully avoid expofing peculiarities and weakneffes, and never engage in the cruel fport of
what

what is called " playing off a character," by leading others to betray their own follies, and make themselves ridiculous without suspecting it. Such an amusement is by no means inconsistent with artificial politeness, because the person who suffers by it is not sensible of the injury; but it is directly contrary to that politeness which is true and sincere, because none of the qualities on which it is founded could ever inspire such conduct, or find any gratification in it. On the contrary, they would give a feeling of the injury, of which the person who suffers it is insensible.

There is indeed something particularly ungenerous in this conduct; it is like a robbery committed in breach of trust; and not only the benevolent, but the honest heart must be shocked at it. To say it is deserved, is no excuse: a punishment may often be deserved, but it can never be a pleasure to a benevolent heart to inflict it.

But it is impossible to enter into a particular detail of the conduct which this *sincere* politeness would inspire on every occasion. Its motive remaining always the same, the manner of expressing it will readily be varied as different circumstances may require; it will observe forms, where a neglect of them would give offence; it will be gentle, mild, and unaffected, at all times;

times; compaffionate, and tenderly attentive to the
afflicted; indulgent to the weak, and ready not only
to bear with them without impatience, but to give
them all poffible affiftance. Ever difpofed to make the
beft of all, eafy, cheerful, and even playful in familiar
intercourfe, and on fuitable occafions; fince, far from
being a reftraint upon the freedom of fociety, it is indeed the only way of throwing afide all reftraint, without
introducing any bad confequences by doing fo.

It needs no artifice or difguife; it purfues no finifter
aims, no felfifh views; but feeks the real good of all,
endeavours to exprefs what it feels, and to appear fuch
as it truly is.

How pleafing were general fociety, if fuch a difpofition prevailed! How delightful all family intercourfe,
if it were never laid afide! Even friendfhip itfelf cannot be compleatly happy without it:—even real affection will not always fupply its place. It is an univerfal
charm, which embellifhes every pleafure in focial life,
prevents numberlefs uneafineffes and difgufts which fo
often difturb its peace, and foftens thofe which it cannot entirely prevent. It adds luftre to every good and
valuable quality, and in fome degree will atone for
many faults, and prevent their bad effects.

But

But it may be afked, how is this quality to be attained? And it muft indeed be owned, that to poffefs it in its utmoft perfection, requires a very fuperior degree both of delicacy and good fenfe, with which all are not endued. But this fhould never difcourage any from the endeavour; for all may improve their talents, if they will exert them, and by aiming at perfection, may make continual advances towards it. Every good quality is beft underftood by endeavouring to practife it.

Let us confider what conduct the fentiments defcribed would dictate on every different occafion; let us endeavour to form to ourfelves the beft notion of it we are able, and then watch for opportunities to put it in practice.

Such an attention will difcover many which were overlooked before; it will fhew us where we have been wanting, and to what caufe it hath been owing; and point out to us thofe qualities in which we are deficient, and which we ought to endeavour to cultivate with the greateft care. Our fphere of action will be enlarged, and many things, too generally confidered as matters of indifference, will become objects of attention, and afford means of improving ourfelves, and benefiting others. Nothing will be neglected as trifling, if it can do this even in the fmalleft degree, fince

in

in that view even trifles become valuable. Our ideas of excellence will be raifed by continually aiming at it, and the heart improved by the thoughts of being thus employed.

Above all, let us fubdue thofe paffions which fo often oppofe what reafon approves, and what would afford the trueft pleafures to the heart; and let us fix all that is good and amiable on the only fure and immoveable foundation—the precepts of that Religion which alone can teach us conftant, univerfal, and difinterefted Benevolence.

ON THE

CHARACTER of CURIO.

"'TIS his way," faid ALCANDER, as CURIO went out of the room: " indeed, my friend, you muft not " mind it, he is an honeft fellow as ever lived."

'It may be fo,' replied HILARIO, ' but really his ' honefty is nothing to me; and had he picked my ' pocket, and converfed with good-humour, I fhould ' have fpent a much more agreeable evening. He has ' done nothing but vent his fpleen againft the world, ' and contradict every thing that was faid; and you ' would have me bear with all this, becaufe he does not ' deferve to be hanged!'

" Indeed," faid ALCANDER, " you do not know " him; with all his roughnefs, he has a worthy, bene- " volent heart;—his family and friends muft bear with " the little peculiarities of his temper, for in effential " things he is always ready to do them fervice, and " I will venture to fay, he would beftow his laft fhil-

" ling

" ling to affift them in diftrefs. I remember, a few
" weeks ago, I met him on the road in a violent rage
" with his fervant, becaufe he had neglected fome
" trifle he expected him to have done; nothing he did
" could pleafe him afterwards, and the poor fellow's
" patience was almoft exhaufted, fo that he was very
" near giving him warning.   Soon after, the fervant's
" horfe threw him, and he was very dangeroufly hurt.
" Curio immediately ran to him, carried him home
" in his arms, fent for the beft affiftance, and attended
" him conftantly himfelf, to fee that he wanted for
" nothing; he paid the whole expence; and as he has
" never recovered fo far as to be able to do his work
" as he did before, Curio has taken care to fpare him
" upon every occafion, and has increafed his wages,
" that he may be able to afford the little indulgences
" he wants."

'How lucky it was,' replied Hilario, 'that the
' poor fellow happened to meet with this terrible acci-
' dent, for otherwife he would never have known that
' he had a good mafter, but might have gone to his
' grave with the opinion that he was an ill-natured
' churl, who cared for nobody but himfelf. The other
' day I met one of his nephews, who had juft been
' at dinner with him; the young fellow was come
' to town from Cambridge for a few days, and had
                                              ' been

' been to vifit his uncle, but happening unfortunately
' to be dreffed for an affembly, the old gentleman was
' difpleafed with his appearance, and began railing at
' the vices and follies of the age, as if his nephew had
' been deeply engaged in them, though I believe no
' one is lefs inclined to them; but every thing he did
' or faid, was wrong through the whole day, and, as he
' has really a refpect for his uncle, he came away quite
' dejected and mortified at his treatment of him.'

" And a few days after," replied ALCANDER,
" when that nephew called to take leave of him, he
" flipt a bank-note of one hundred pounds into his
" hands at parting, to pay the expences of his journey,
" and ran out of the room to avoid receiving his
" thanks for it."

' So then,' returned HILARIO, ' if the young man
' is of a fordid difpofition, and thinks money a better
' thing than friendfhip, good-humour, and all the
' amiable qualities which render life agreeable, he has
' reafon to be perfectly fatisfied with his uncle; if he
' is not, the old gentleman has done his part to make
' him fo, by fhewing him, that, according to his no-
' tions, kindnefs confifts in giving money. For my
' part, if ever I fhould be a beggar, or break my bones,
' I may perhaps be glad to meet with your friend
' again;

' again; but as I hope neither of thofe things are ever
' likely to happen to me, I am by no means ambitious
' of the honour of his acquaintance:—his good qua-
' lities are nothing to me, and his bad ones are a
' plague to all who come in his way.'

" One may bear with them," replied ALCANDER,
" where there is fo much real worth: the whole world
" could not bribe that man to do a bafe action."

' So much the better for him,' returned HILARIO;
' but really, as I faid before, it is nothing to me; and
' after all, whatever excufes your good-nature may
' find for him, there muft be fomething wrong in the
' heart, where the manners are fo unpleafant.'

" He has not a good temper," faid ALCANDER,
" and every man has not the fame command over
" himfelf; but indeed he has a good heart; and if
" you knew him as well as I do, you muft love him
" with all his oddities."

' His oddities are quite enough for me,' returned
HILARIO, ' and I defire to know no more of him; he
' might make me *efteem* him, but he could never
' make me *love* him; and it is very unpleafant to feel
' one of thefe, where one cannot feel the other.'

ALCANDER

ALCANDER could not but be fenfible of the truth of many of HILARIO's obfervations;—he fighed in fecret for the friend whofe good qualities he valued, and whofe foibles gave him pain; and could CURIO have known what his friend felt for him at that moment, it might perhaps have gone farther than all he ever read or thought upon the fubject, towards correcting a fault for which he often blamed himfelf, but which he ftill continued to indulge, and to imagine himfelf unable to fubdue.

Perhaps neither of the parties concerned in this difpute were well qualified to judge as to the fubject of it. Efteem and regard influenced the one, and added ftrength to his good-nature; while the other, whofe patience was wearied out by the ill-humours of a ftranger, of whofe merits he was ignorant, was naturally difpofed to view them in an unfavourable light.   But fuch a converfation muft induce every indifferent perfon to reflect on the importance of a quality which could oblige a friend to blufh for the perfon he efteemed, and make an enemy at firft fight of one by no means wanting in good-nature, who came into company with a difpofition to pleafe and to be pleafed, and whofe difguft was occafioned by a difappointment in that aim.

Can

Can fuch a quality be a matter of little confequence, which thofe who are punctual in their duty in more effential points may be permitted to neglect? Can it be a difpofition fo ftrongly implanted in the heart of any man, that his utmoft efforts cannot conquer it?— The firft fuppofition might furnifh an excufe for giving way to any fault, fince all may fancy they have virtues to counterbalance it. The laft would reduce us almoft to mere machines, and difcourage every effort to reform and improve the heart, without which no real and folid virtue can be attained.

FORTITUDE.

TRUE Fortitude is a ftrength of mind, which cannot be overcome by any trials or any fufferings. It confifts not in being infenfible of them, for there is no real fortitude in bearing what we do not feel; but it renders us fuperior to them, and enables us to act as we ought to do in every different fituation in life, in every change that can affect our outward circumftances, or our inward feelings.

There is a kind of fortitude which proceeds from natural conftitution; fome are lefs affected by trials than others; and fome, from ftrong health and fpirits, are able to go through a great deal without finking under it. But this can only extend to a certain degree. Afflictions may come to fuch a height, that the moft infenfible muft feel them; and then their apparent fortitude is overcome, and the ftrongeft health and fpirits can only refift a little longer than the weakeft,

—they

—they muſt give way to a ſufficient force, and therefore can never be the ſource of true and conſtant fortitude.

There is alſo a kind of fortitude which is called forth into action on particular occaſions, and for a time appears ſuperior to the trial; and this may ſometimes be inſpired even by motives which are in themſelves highly blameable. A point in view which is eagerly purſued, will enable a perſon to go through what at other times might appear inſupportable; but this can only laſt while the motive remains in force; and thoſe who by this have been rendered equal to what appear to be the greateſt trials, have often at other times ſunk under the ſmalleſt. True fortitude muſt ſpring from ſome principle which is conſtant and unchangeable, and can ſupport it at all times, and againſt every attack.

It cannot therefore be derived from any thing in this world. Natural ſtrength muſt yield to pain and ſorrow;—earthly conſiderations can ſupport us no farther than their immediate influence extends:—pride cannot enable us to bear humiliations, or even thoſe little mortifications which daily occur, when there is no credit to be gained by doing ſo;—and philoſophy muſt at laſt be reduced to nothing more than ſuppreſſing complaints; and making the beſt of what it cannot cure.

cure. Thefe may infpire a ftrength which will laft for a time—a ftrength which may ferve for certain occafions, but will fail on others; or an appearance of ftrength to conceal our weaknefs. But none of thefe can infpire that fortitude which is a conftant invariable difpofition of mind, prepared for every trial, and fuperior to them all. This can only be derived from a confidence in that affiftance which can never fail; from a motive for action which is fufficient to carry us through every trial; and from hopes which nothing in this world can take away.

The effect of this fortitude is, that it makes us fteadily and conftantly purfue the great aim we have in view; it is drawn afide by no pleafure; it fhrinks at no difficulty; it finks under no affliction; but refolutely goes on, whatever may be the path affigned, and though it may fuffer, it never yields.

This virtue is exercifed, not only in the greateft afflictions, but in the daily occurrences of life; and if in thefe its trials are not fo painful, yet they may perhaps often be more difficult. It enables us to bear the faults and weakneffes of others, the difappointments and humiliations which all muft meet with, and the numberlefs little vexations and inconveniencies, which though when confidered feparately they may appear trifling,

J.   yet

yet often affect the temper much more than we are generally aware of.

It is alfo exercifed by our own weakneffes and imperfections; for there is no perfon living who can always preferve the fame equal ftate of mind and fpirits; and it is no inconfiderable part of true fortitude, to avoid giving way to what none can avoid feeling; and to perfevere in acting as we ought in every different difpofition of mind.

This then is the great and diftinguifhing character of true fortitude;—That it is conftant and invariable, the fame at all times, in all trials, and in all difpofitions; it depends not on the circumftances in which we may be placed, nor on the ftrength either of body or fpirits which we may enjoy; but it enables us to exert all the ftrength we poffefs, (which is often much more than we are apt to imagine) it is feated in the will, and never gives way in any inftance.

Without this virtue, there can be no dependance on any other. Thofe who have the beft inclinations in the world, muft find a time of difficulty; a time when, from the oppofition they may meet with, or from their own weaknefs, the performance of their duty muft require no fmall degree of exertion; and if they have

not

not fortitude to go on, in fpite of all fuch difficulties, their former good difpofitions and good actions will be of little ufe.

The practice of virtue is indeed often attended with applaufe fufficient to animate vanity to affume the appearance of it; and even where it is pure and genuine, the efteem and affection engaged by it, cannot but be highly pleafing to all, and muft afford fome degree of affiftance and fupport. But there are many inftances in which all thefe fupports are entirely wanting; and true fortitude will enable us to act as we ought to do without any fuch affiftance, and even when we are fure that the confequence of doing fo will be directly contrary to all this.

It can bear not only the want of approbation, but the mortification of being flighted or blamed, and perfevere, whatever may be the confequence in regard to this world: not from a contempt for the opinions of others, for it does not hinder fuch humiliations from being felt, but it fupports them with courage and refolution, and will never endeavour to avoid them by the flighteft deviation from the right path, or to return them by a difplay of its fuperiority, or by giving any degree of pain or humiliation to thofe from whom they came. Far from being a ftern or rugged quality, it is

indifpen-

indifpenfably neceffary to fupport that gentlenefs and fweetnefs of difpofition, which form the charm of focial life, and which can never be long preferved by thofe who have not fortitude to bear the vexations they muft often meet with from the weakneffes and inadvertencies, and even from the pride and ill-temper, of thofe with whom they converfe; that *fpirit*, (as it is commonly called) which immediately refents every trifling injury, and endeavours to return it, is in fact a weaknefs,—a proof of not being able to bear them. True fortitude can conquer it; and without this, no apparent gentlenefs of character can ever be depended on, fince it will only laft till there is fufficient provocation to get the better of it.

To the want of this kind of fortitude, much of the unhappinefs of fociety is owing. A trifle gives offence, and is refented; we cannot bear a little mortification, or humiliation; or, perhaps, we cannot bear to appear to want fpirit to refent fuch things, and do ourfelves juftice. True fortitude can bear it all, whenever it is our duty to do fo; and few confider the importance of exerting it on fuch occafions.

It enables us to acknowledge our errors and our faults, inftead of having recourfe to any artifice or mifreprefentation to difguife or juftify what the heart

in

in fecret difapproves, or muft difapprove, on a fair and impartial confideration; to which, want of fortitude to bear the mortifying view of our own imperfections, is often one of the greateft hindrances.

In great afflictions, fortitude is exerted not only in fuppreffing complaints and murmurs, but in rendering us fuperior to them, by enabling us to take an enlarged view of things; to confider the hand from which they come, and the advantages which may be derived from them; and it infpires not merely a tame fubmiffion, but an active refolution, which in every trial exerts its utmoft powers, and excites us to do the beft we can, whatever that may be, and whatever ftruggle fuch exertion may coft us.

In fhort, it enables us to make the beft of every thing, to purfue fteadily and conftantly the path of duty, unmoved by all the attacks of pleafure or of pain, and unwearied by the moft tedious and apparently unfuccefsful exertions.

In order to obtain this fortitude, we cannot but be fenfible, that a ftrength fuperior to our own is neceffary; the experience of every day muft fhew us our weaknefs, and the infufficiency of thofe fupports which any thing in this world can afford us. But the Word of Eter-

nal

nal Truth has promifed us a help which fhall never fail thofe who fincerely feek for it: for this then we muft apply by conftant prayer, not only in general, but in every particular inftance. But we muft not fuppofe that this help can be obtained without exerting our own endeavours; we muft do our beft, that we may hope to be affifted; and in fo doing, we may fecurely depend upon it, in every trial that can come upon us.

Too great a confidence in our own ftrength is, indeed, directly contrary to true fortitude, and generally leads to a defeat; but we fhould alfo be cautious that we do not run into another extreme, and give way to fuch a degree of diffidence as may hinder us from exerting ourfelves, or give the name of diffidence to real indolence.

The confcioufnefs of our own weaknefs fhould, indeed, induce us to feek a more powerful affiftance, but our endeavours are neceffary in order to obtain it; and neither the prefumptuous, nor the indolent, have any right to hope for it.

Let us, then, exert ourfelves on every occafion, and never give way in the fmalleft inftance, if we mean to be fteady in the greateft. Let us endeavour to imprefs upon our minds the importance of the objects we have

in

in view—the favour of GOD, and our own eternal
happinefs; we fhall then have a motive for action
continually before us, fufficient to fupport us in the
greateft difficulties, to arm us againft the fevereft
fhocks of affliction, and enable us to endure the longeft courfe of fufferings to which human life is liable.

Is it poffible we fhould fink under the humiliation
we may meet with from this world, while we may
hope for the approbation of GOD himfelf? Can we
not fuffer tranfitory affliction, with the profpect of
endlefs felicity before us?——It is for want of attending fufficiently to thefe things, that prefent trials appear
to us fo infupportable; and the only effectual preparation for thefe trials is, to arm ourfelves with comforts
which they cannot take away, and motives for action
which may be fufficient to carry us through them with
refolution and vigour.

When we look into the Holy Scriptures, we find the
Chriftian life continually reprefented as a ftate of warfare, in which we are called to contend with the
temptations of this world, and with our own perverfe
inclinations. We muft deny ourfelves, and take up
the crofs, if we would be the difciples of Chrift;—we
muft conquer, if we would obtain the crown;—we
muft lay afide every weight, and run with patience the

race

race that is set before us;—we must endure unto the end, if we hope to be saved.

Such is the account given us of the state to which we are called, and such a prospect must strongly impress upon our minds the necessity of arming ourselves with true fortitude;—of being stedfast, immoveable, while we have the most powerful and comfortable motives to induce us to be so;—forasmuch as we *know* that our " labour is not vain in the Lord." We know that we shall conquer if we faint not; that if we are faithful unto death, He will give us a crown of life—a happiness beyond what the eye hath seen, or the ear heard, or the heart of man is able to conceive.

Such a view of the Christian state must shew us, in a strong light, the nature of that fortitude that is required, in order to enable us to perform our part in it. Human motives may inspire occasional exertions which excite admiration; but those instances of fortitude which are most admired, are seldom, in reality, such as are most difficult; and the true Christian must be armed with a fortitude far superior to that which is displayed on such occasions; a fortitude which requires no earthly support; which aims at no present reward; which resists pleasure and pain, humiliation and weariness; which is the same at all times, and can always

obtain

obtain the moft difficult of all conquefts—that which is gained over our own inclinations.

The perfon who facrifices pleafure to ambition, convenience to avarice, or any prefent indulgence to pride, or fome other predominant paffion, may appear to act with fortitude in many inftances, when, in fact, his conduct is directly contrary to it; fince he only gives way to a darling inclination, and purfues the means of gratifying it; and fhould a trial come which required the facrifice of that inclination, his imaginary fortitude muft fail.

But the fortitude of the true Chriftian is prepared for every thing; like all his other virtues, it is not the oc-cafional exertion of a moment, but the conftant difpo-fition of his mind. It is alfo, like all other virtues, never perfectly known, but by endeavouring to practife it. All are fenfible that it is neceffary in pain and af-flictions : few confider fufficiently how often it is ne-ceffary even in the moft ordinary occurrences—the moft trifling converfations.

How often are the real fentiments difguifed, the in-nocent injured, and falfe maxims fuffered to gain ground, merely for want of refolution to refift the tor-rent, from a fear of being fingular, or of lofing any

fhare

share in the good opinion of others by opposing their sentiments! And thus the cause of truth and goodness is betrayed, and often suffers as much from timid friends as from real enemies; for conversation will influence the character and conduct: by degrees the mind grows familiar with what once it disapproved, and learns to believe what has been frequently repeated, and suffered to pass unnoticed, till that delicacy, which was shocked at the least appearance of any thing wrong, is insensibly worn away.

Wrong opinions mislead the practice, and uncharitable ones corrupt the heart; but those exertions which true fortitude inspires, should at the same time be carefully distinguished from that positiveness and love for contradiction which so often disturb the peace and pleasure of society, and which (even when they happen to be exerted in a good cause) frequently do a real injury to what they mean to defend.

The person who feels pain in opposing the opinions and inclinations of others, and does it merely from a sense of duty, will always endeavour to avoid giving pain by doing so; but a gentleness and timidity of disposition, and an earnest desire to please, are qualities which may lead to excesses, as well as the contrary; and true fortitude requires the sacrifice of our inclinations, whenever our duty makes it necessary.

But it is impoffible to enumerate the various inftances in which fortitude is neceffary in the daily occurrences of life. A careful attention to our own
conduct, and a candid enquiry into the motives of it,
will be the fureft means to point out to us wherein we
are wanting, and to give us a juft notion of that fortitude which is neceffary to fupport us on every different
occafion.

Let us then often examine our own hearts, and enquire
whether the fear of difpleafing others does not fometimes
induce us to difguife our real fentiments, and appear to
approve what in our hearts we condemn ? —Whether
we are not fometimes pofitive, becaufe we cannot bear
to own ourfelves in the wrong; or complying, becaufe
we dread being thought fo ?—Whether we do not
fometimes give a fanction to uncertain fufpicions, or
ill-natured ridicule, from a fear of being thought to
poffefs lefs penetration than others, or from the apprehenfion of expofing ourfelves to the like, if we fhould
venture to oppofe them?—In fhort, whether we are
never induced by fear, either to fpeak, or to be filent,
when our own unprejudiced judgement would have
led us to do otherwife? If fo, we are, in that inftance,
wanting in true fortitude ; nor is the want of it lefs
evident in giving way to our own faults and weakneffes,
than to thofe of others.

Can

Can we fubdue our pride, anger, fretfulnefs, &c.—
all thofe paffions which are fo often excited by trifles
in common life, and which, on fuch occafions, are in
general too eafily fuffered to take their courfe without
refiftance? Do we not rather fometimes give way to
them, for want of refolution to endeavour to fupprefs
them; or from a fear of being defpifed for our infenfibility, or our tamenefs, if we fhould fuffer any injury to
pafs unnoticed? Can we bear the various kinds of
mortifications we may meet with from others, without
endeavouring to return them; and fubmit even to unjuft cenfure, when charity or any other duty requires
our doing fo? Can we facrifice our inclinations to thofe
of others, with cheerfulnefs and good-humour, without
telling the world that we are doing fo, and endeavouring to exalt ourfelves at the expence of thofe we pretend to oblige, and to gain admiration to fupport and
reward us? Can we bear the follies and weaknefles
of thofe with whom we converfe, and the many little
circumftances which often render fociety tirefome to us,
without giving pain by fhewing that it is fo? And do
we endeavour, by every gentle and engaging method,
not only to make others eafy and happy, but to win
them over to all that is amiable and good, and help
them to amend thofe imperfections which we cannot
help obferving, without expofing them to the humiliation of knowing that we are fenfible of them?——
                                                    The

'The good that may be done in this way is feldom attended to as it deferves; but fuch endeavours require no fmall degree of fortitude, fince their fuccefs muft, in general, be attained by flow and almoft imperceptible degrees, and often remains entirely unknown; and far from being attended with any admiration, they will, for the moft part, pafs unnoticed—perhaps often be totally mifinterpreted.

Thefe are but few of the numberlefs occafions in which true fortitude is neceffary in common life. A little attention to the circumftances which daily occur, will point out to us many more, on which it may be highly ufeful to enquire into the motives of our conduct; and fuch enquiries will often fhew, that want of fortitude is in reality the fource of many faults and imperfections, which are too generally overlooked, or afcribed to fome other caufe.

How happy then is the fituation of him who is armed with that true and conftant fortitude, which refts with full confidence on Almighty Power, and is fupported by it in every trial:—who is thus prepared for all events, and able not only to *fuffer*, but to *act* as he ought to do in every different fituation;—who can bear with the fame refolution thofe fevere fhocks which at once deftroy his earthly happinefs, and thofe little mortifi-

mortifications which continually allay it;—who never can be deterred from the path of duty, either by the allurements of pleafure, the dread of fufferings, or the wearinefs and difguft which attend on long-continued trials, and the difcouragement of repeated difappointments!

The nerves may tremble at the approach of pain,—the fpirits may fink beneath a load of grief,—but the refolution remains unmoved; and pain or affliction, however ftrongly felt, are boldly encountered, whenever they are inflicted by the difpenfations of Providence, or when the confideration of duty makes it neceffary voluntarily to endure them.

This alone is true Chriftian Fortitude;—a fortitude far fuperior to that which in many ftriking inftances has engaged the admiration of mankind:—and this is neceffary to all who wifh to attain that perfection to which we are called.

CANDOUR.

THERE are many people who take the meafure of a character like the taylor in Laputa, who, in order to make a fuit of clothes for Gulliver, took the fize of his thumb, and concluded that the reft was in proportion: they form their judgement from fome flight circumftance, and conclude that the reft of the character muft be of a piece with it.

Were all bodies formed according to the exact rules of proportion, this method of taking the meafure would be infallible, fuppofing the taylor perfectly acquainted with thofe rules ; but in order to find the fame certainty in this method of judging of characters, we muft not only fuppofe, that the perfon who is to judge of them is equally well informed of all the different variations ; but we muft alfo fuppofe, that the fame motives regularly produce the fame actions, and that the fame feelings are always expreffed in the fame manner. A very

very little obfervation is fufficient to fhew that this is
far from being the cafe.

Human nature, it is faid, is always the fame. But
what is human nature?—and who could ever enumerate all its various powers, inclinations, affections,
and paffions, with all the different effects they may
produce by their different combinations; the objects on
which they may be employed, and the variety of circumftances which may attend them.

This leaves a wide field for imagination to exert itfelf.
But attention and obfervation might ferve to perplex
and make us diffident of our own judgement; and as
it is much eafier, as well as more flattering to vanity,
to judge from a firft impreffion, than from reafon and
reflection, a favourable or unfavourable prejudice is apt
to take the lead in the opinions formed of the actions
of thofe about whom we are much interefted. Where
this is not the cafe, moft people meafure by a certain line
of their own, beyond which they know not how to go;
and when they meet with refinements of which they
are incapable, they can form no idea of them in another;
and therefore, by affigning fome other motive to fuch
actions, they reduce them to their own ftandard; and
being then able to comprehend what was unintelli-
gible before, they conclude that their prefent opinion
muft

muſt certainly be right, and form their judgment of the reſt of the character according to it.

From theſe and many other cauſes which might be aſſigned, it appears, that there muſt always be great uncertainty in the opinions we form of the actions of others, and in the inferences we draw from particular actions concerning the general character. The obvious concluſion from which is, that we ſhould be always upon our guard againſt forming an haſty judgment, or laying too much ſtreſs upon thoſe judgments which we cannot help forming; and be very cautious that we do not ſuffer our own prejudices and fancies acquire the force of truth, and influence our opinions afterwards.

Yet ſtill, whilſt we live in this world, and converſe with others, it is impoſſible to avoid forming ſome opinion of them from their words and actions; and it is not always eaſy to aſcertain the juſt bounds within which this opinion ought to be confined, and to diſtinguiſh between the dictates of reaſon, and thoſe of prejudice and imagination.

Since then we cannot ſhut our eyes, it may be uſeful to us to procure as much light as we can; not that we may be continually prying into what does not con-

M   cern

cern us, but that where we cannot avoid forming some judgment, we may do it with juftice and candour : that we may learn to avoid being pofitive, where we muſt be uncertain; and to fee and confefs our error, where we may have been wrong.

A benevolent heart, ever defirous of confidering the actions of others in the moſt favourable light, will indeed be lefs liable than any other to the bad confequences which may follow from the difficulties attending on our judgments of others : for an error on the favourable fide is far lefs pernicious to them, or to ourfelves, than the contrary would be; yet every error is liable to bad confequences. The perfon who has formed an hafty favourable judgment, may probably in time be convinced of his miſtake: having been deceived, he may grow fufpicious, till every appearance of good is miſtruſted, and he falls by degrees into the contrary extreme : for error cannot be the foundation of real and laſting good, fince, fooner or later, it muſt be ſhaken; and then the fuperſtructure, however beautiful in appearance, will fall to ruins.

True Charity and Benevolence certainly do not confiſt in deceiving ourfelves and others; they do not make us blind and infenfible, nor do they give a falfe light, to lead us aſtray from the truth, and then leave

us

us bewildered in darknefs and error, feeking in vain to return, and miftrufting every appearance of light which would conduct us back again. Like all other virtues, they flow from the Source of Eternal Truth; they muft be firmly rooted in the heart, and continually exercifed in every different fituation, not merely the tranfient effects of fpirits and good-humour, which fometimes make a perfon difpofed to be pleafed with others, only becaufe he is pleafed with himfelf; for then he will be difpleafed again with as little reafon, whenever the prefent humour gives place to another. Still lefs are they the effect of weaknefs of judgment, and want of difcernment and penetration; which, in fact, are more likely to lead to the contrary extreme. —That they are fometimes confidered in this laft point of view, may perhaps be one of the chief rea- fons for that want of them, which fo often appears in general converfation.

The vanity of difplaying fuperior talents is very pre valent, and it is often much more from this principle, than from real ill-nature, that the faults and imperfec- tions of the abfent are expofed. To gain admiration is the object of purfuit: any other way by which it might be attained, would anfwer the purpofe juft as well; but unfortunately all others are more difficult, while this is within the reach of all; for the weakeft

have

have penetration enough to difcover imperfections in
thofe whofe excellencies are far above their reach.

Thofe who have no folid virtues of their own may
affume a temporary fuperiority, by declaiming againft
the faults of others; and thofe who have neither wit,
nor any talents to amufe, may yet raife a laugh by expofing what is ridiculous, or may be made to appear
fo.   A little more of that penetration which they are
fo defirous of being thought to poffefs, might help to a
farther infight into themfelves and others; they might
perhaps find that they have only been expofing what
was obvious to every body, and gaining the reputation
of ill-nature, in fact without deferving it, (any otherwife than by inattention;) for admiration was their
point in view; and it is very poffible that the confequences of what they faid, might never enter their
thoughts; and that they would have been really fhocked,
had they confidered them in their true light.   But
raifing themfelves, not depreciating others, was the
object of their purfuit; and the means of attaining it
were confidered merely as fuch, without any attention
to their confequences.

Perhaps fome rigid cenfor, who heard the converfation, may fall into an error of the fame kind with
their own; and, for want of fufficiently penetrating
their

their motives, may fuppofe them loft to all fenfe of candour and benevolence, and actuated folely by ma-lice and ill-nature; while a perfon of real difcernment would have avoided the errors of both; and not from weaknefs, but from ftrength of judgment, would have acted a more charitable part; for nothing is more juft than the obfervation of an excellent author: " Ce n'eft " point au depens de l'efprit qu'on eft bon." The faults and follies are often the moft obvious parts of a character, while many good qualities remain unnoticed by the generality of the world, unlefs fome extraordi-nary occafion call them forth to action.

It is wonderful to obferve, how many unfavourable and unjuft opinions are formed, merely by not fuffici-ently confidering the very different lights in which the fame action will appear to different perfons on different occafions. How many things are faid in general con-verfation, from thoughtlefsnefs and inattention, from a flow of fpirits, and a defire to fay fomething, which will not ftand the teft of a fevere cenfure, and which, confidered feparately, may appear in fuch a light as the fpeaker never thought of! Not only the ill-natured, but the fuperficial obferver may often be mifled by fuch appearances, and fhocked at things which want only to be underftood in order to fecure them a more favourable judgement.

M 3   The

The difpofition of the hearer, as well as that of the fpeaker, may alfo contribute greatly to make things appear different from what they really are; and great allowances fhould be made for his own paffions and prejudices, as well as for thofe of others; for though they may be fuppofed to be better known to him, yet it is evident that every one, while under their immediate influence, is very ill qualified to judge how far they may affect his opinions.

A perfon who is under any particular dejection of fpirits, and feels that a kind word or look would be a cordial to his heart, may be overcome by the mirth of a cheerful fociety, and inclined to attribute to infenfibility what perhaps was merely owing to ignorance of his fituation, and the lively impreffion of prefent pleafure: while another, whofe heart is elated by fome little fuccefs which his imagination has raifed far above its real value, may be fhocked at the coldnefs of thofe, who, being more rational and lefs interefted, fee the matter in its true light, and therefore cannot fhare in his joy in the manner he expects and wifhes.

What multitudes of unfavourable and unjuft opinions would be at once removed, if we could put ourfelves in the place of others, and fee things in the light in which they appear to them,—the only way of
forming

forming a right eſtimate of their conduct in regard to
them. But while we judge of the actions of others by
our own feelings, or rather by our own reaſonings,
upon what we chooſe to ſuppoſe would be our feelings
on the like occaſion, we muſt be liable to continual
miſtakes.

To feel for others, is a quality generally claimed by
all, and which certainly in ſome degree ſeems to be
implanted in human nature. They muſt be infenſible
indeed, or ſomething far worſe, who can ſee others
happy, without being pleaſed; or miſerable, without
ſympathiſing in their ſufferings, and wiſhing to relieve
them. But to enter fully into the feelings of others,
to be truly ſenſible of the impreſſion every circum-
ſtance makes in their ſituation, is much more difficult,
and more uncommon, than at firſt ſight may appear;
and yet, unleſs we could do this, there muſt always be
great uncertainty in our opinions of their conduct; and
it may afford no ſmall ſatisfaction to a perſon of true
benevolence, when he feels the pain of being obliged to
think unfavourably of another, to conſider at the ſame
time, that if he knew all, he might find many reaſons
to abate the ſeverity of the cenſure which he hears
pronounced by others, and to which he is unable to
give a ſatisfactory anſwer, becauſe, according to appearances, it ſeems to have been deſerved.

Moſt

Moſt people act much more from their feelings, than from reaſon and reflection;—thoſe who conſider coolly of circumſtances in which they are no way intereſted, may lay a plan of conduct which may appear to them ſo rational and natural, that they wonder how any one could miſs it; while thoſe who are engaged in action, are often hurried on by the impulſe of the preſent moment, and, without having any bad intention, may fall into ſuch errors as the cool reaſoner would think almoſt impoſſible; or perhaps ſometimes, without conſidering the matter, they may riſe to heights of excellence which would never have occurred to him, and which, for that reaſon, he may probably be unable to comprehend, and therefore very liable to miſinterpret.

It may generally be obſerved, that in every ſcience a ſlight and ſuperficial knowledge often makes a perſon vain and poſitive; while long and attentive ſtudy, and a deep inſight into the real nature of things, produce a contrary effect, and lead to humility and diffidence. This may be partly owing to that deſire of diſplaying what they poſſeſs, which is often found in thoſe who poſſeſs but little, and are therefore ambitious of making the moſt of it, in order to impoſe upon the world by falſe appearances, and prevent a diſcovery of that poverty which they wiſh to conceal; but it is alſo often owing to a real miſapprehenſion of things.

The

The fuperficial obferver confiders the object only in one point of view, which perhaps is new to him, and therefore ftrikes his imagination ftrongly; and it does not occur to him that it may be confidered in other lights, and that, upon farther enquiry, he might find reafon to change his opinion, or at leaft to doubt of what at firft appeared to him clear and evident. Pleafed with what he has acquired, and ignorant of what farther might be acquired, he is fatisfied and pofitive; while thofe who are farther advanced, fee a vaft field of knowledge open before them, of which they are fenfible that they can explore only a very fmall part; and by taking an enlarged view of things, and obferving how often they have been deceived by confidering them in a falfe light, are taught to avoid being pofitive, where they are fenfible their knowledge is imperfect.

This may be applied to the ftudy of the human heart, as well as to every other, in which we can only judge from appearances. Thofe who know leaft are often moft ready to decide, and moft pofitive in their decifions; and pofitivenefs generally gains more credit than it deferves. The confequences of this are perhaps more pernicious in regard to this fubject than any other, becaufe it requires much lefs penetration to difcover faults and weakneffes, than real and folid good qualities. From hence may appear the injuftice of fuppofing,

that

that perfons of deep knowledge and obfervation of mankind are to be avoided, as being inclined to pafs the fevereft judgments on the conduct of others.   Thofe indeed who harbour any criminal defigns, and conceal vice under the mafk of hypocrify, may tremble under the eye of a keen obferver; for fuch an one may fee through their deepeft difguifes, and expofe them in their true light when it is neceffary, in order to prevent the mifchief they might do.   He may alfo detect the fallacy of an affumed merit, and falfe virtue, which have paffed upon the world for real; but he will fee at the fame time the allowances which candour may make for every fault and weaknefs.   He will difcover many an humble excellence which feeks not to difplay itfelf to the world, and many an inftance of true goodnefs of heart, and delicacy of fentiment, expreffed in trifling circumftances, which would pafs unobferved, or perhaps be totally mifinterpreted, by a perfon of lefs obfervation and knowledge of mankind.   He will alfo be more open to conviction, and ready to acknowledge a miftake, becaufe he is not under the neceffity of endeavouring to impofe upon the world by a falfe appearance of knowledge, which always indicates a deficiency in what is true and genuine.

Ignorance alone pretends to infallibility.   A perfon of real knowledge is fenfible that he muft be liable to
                                              error,

error, and has not the fame reafon to be afraid of acknowledging it in any particular inftance; and if his
knowledge be joined with true benevolence, he will be
continually watching for an opportunity to change his
opinion, if that opinion has been formed on the unfavourable fide, or at leaft to difcover fome good qualities
which may counterbalance the fault he could not help
obferving. For the fame reafons, he will be always
ready and willing to obferve an alteration for the better
in thofe of whom he has thought moft unfavourably,
inftead of being glad (as is fometimes the cafe with
others) of any new inftance which may ferve to confirm
the opinion formerly pronounced, and afraid of any
thing which may contradict it. He will always remember, that the worft character may improve; and
the fevereft judgments ever pronounced by the ignorant
and ill-natured, even thofe which have been affented to
with regret by the fenfible and benevolent, may afterwards be changed : but the firft will be afraid and unwilling to acknowledge, that they have been obliged to
change their opinion; the laft will be ever ready to do
it, and not afhamed to own it, when they can obferve
a change of conduct.

Knowledge is indeed quick-fighted, but ignorance
is improperly reprefented as being blind; it rather furnifhes a falfe light, which leads into a thoufand errors
and

and miftakes. The difference between them does not confift in the number of their obfervations, but in the truth and juftnefs of them. Penetration may difcover thofe faults and weakneffes which really exift, but ignorance will fancy it has difcovered many which never exifted at all; and it is difficult indeed to convince ignorance of a miftake.

It may alfo be obferved, that thofe qualities which difpofe us to make a right ufe of the knowledge of mankind, contribute at the fame time to increafe that knowledge.

The heart which is merely felfifh does not underftand the language of benevolence, difinterestednefs, and generofity, and therefore is very liable to misinterpret it; while thofe who feel themfelves capable of great and worthy actions, will find no difficulty in believing that others may be fo too, and will have an idea of a character which can hardly ever be perfectly underftood by thofe who feel nothing like it in themfelves.

Vice, even in fpite of itfelf, muft pay a reverence to virtue, confidered in general; but the moft exalted heights, and moft refined inftances of it, are far above its comprehenfion.

This

This obſervation holds not only in regard to ſuch characters as are entirely abandoned to vice, but to all the leſſer degrees of it; which always, more or leſs, tend to inſpire ſuſpicion, and make it difficult to underſtand an oppoſite character, or believe it to be ſuch as to an honeſt and good heart it would immediately appear.

It is impoſſible to read or hear the obſervations of thoſe who are celebrated for the deepeſt knowledge of mankind, without being hurt to obſerve, that vice and folly, with the means of playing upon them, and making advantage of them, are made the general objects of attention; while true goodneſs of heart, and rectitude of character, are hardly ever mentioned. And yet, if ſuch things can exiſt, (and what muſt his heart be who believes they do not) he who leaves them entirely out in his account, muſt have but an imperfect knowledge of mankind.

Another way in which a ſlight and ſuperficial knowledge of mankind is very apt to miſlead, is that love of reducing every thing to general rules, which is always found in thoſe whoſe views are not very extenſive. A few ſuch rules are eaſily remembered; and they have an appearance of conveying a great deal of knowledge at once, which often procures them a favourable

vourable reception, not only from thofe who are defirous of concealing their ignorance under an appearance
of knowledge, but even from fuch as might be capable
of detecting their fallacy, if they would give themfelves
the trouble of examining them.

To fay that all men act from pride, felf-intereft, &c.
and then to explain every action accordingly, is much
eafier than to trace the motives of different actions in
different characters, and difcover the various fources
from whence they fpring; and this is much more flattering to vanity, than to acknowledge ourfelves unable to
explain them.

A general rule, which has been found to anfwer in
fome inftances, is a moft valuable acquifition to thofe
who talk more than they think, and are more defirous of the appearance of knowledge and penetration,
than of the reality; and fuch rules are often repeated
from one to another, without being fufficiently examined, till they gain the force of truth, and are received
as maxims, which it would be thought unreafonable
to controvert.

The neceffity of ufing metaphorical language, to exprefs the fentiments of the heart, may perhaps often
have given occafion to miftakes of this kind; the qua-
                                                      lities

lities which belong to the literal fenfe of the word are applied to it when ufed metaphorically; and from a habit of connecting the word with thofe qualities, fuch reafonings often pafs current, though a little attention might eafily have difcovered the miftake on which they are founded. This is ftill more likely to happen when the fame metaphor is ufed to exprefs different fentiments, which from the poverty of language upon fuch fubjects muft fometimes happen.

The words *warmth* and *heat*, (for example) originally denoting the properties of fire, have been metaphorically ufed to exprefs thofe of affection, and thofe of anger or refentment. This circumftance alone has probably given rife to an obfervation often repeated, and very generally received, "that a warm friend will "be equally warm in his anger and refentment, and "confequently will be a bitter enemy." It would be juft as rational to fay, "he will burn your fingers;" for it is only from reafoning upon words without ideas, that either the one or the other can be afferted.

That tender affectionate difpofition, which conftitutes the character of a warm friend, and difpofes him even to forget himfelf for the fake of the object beloved, is not more different from the qualities of natural fire, than from that proud and felfifh fpirit which infpires
violent

violent anger and refentment. To the firſt, (according to the expreſſion of an elegant writer) " la haine feroit " un tourment;" but the laſt finds his ſatisfaction (if that word can ever be applied to ſuch a character) in the indulgence of his hatred, and the endeavour to exprefs it.

A very little attention to the real qualities of thefe characters, might ſurely be ſufficient to ſhew that they are widely different; though the habit of uſing the ſame words to exprefs them, has led to an habitual connection of the ideas, and prevents this difference from ſtriking us at firſt ſight.

The ſame would be found to be the cafe in many other inſtances, where general obfervations have been received, merely becaufe they found plauſibly, and are repeated ſo often that they are believed of courfe, without enquiring into the truth and juſtice of them. And when ſuch are made the ground-work of the judgments formed in particular inſtances, thoſe judgments muſt be liable to numberlefs errors, which will eafily gain ground, becaufe they favour a received opinion.

That this method of judging by general rules, on fubjects ſo various and complicated as the difpofitions of the human heart, is very liable to error, ſhould
alone

alone be fufficient to put us on our guard againft it; but there is an additional reafon for this, from the probability that they may be founded on obfervations drawn from the moft unfavourable views of human nature; the effects of bad qualities being, in general, more extenfive and more apparent than thofe of good ones; fince the laft are frequently employed in preventing mifchief, and they are fcarce ever taken notice of. They alfo make the deepeft impreffion; for all are fenfible of the evils they have fuffered; few pay fufficient attention to thofe they have efcaped.

Whenever, therefore, the application of a general rule difpofes us to an unfavourable judgment in any particular inftance, that circumftance fhould render it fufpected, and make us lefs ready to admit the conclufions which may be drawn from it.

This again may ferve to fhew, that perfons of enlarged views and extenfive knowledge are far from being on that account difpofed to be fevere; but on the contrary, if they make a right ufe of them, will thereby be enabled to correct the errors of others, and be led to a more candid and liberal way of judging than the reft of the world.

N   They

They cannot indeed retain that difpofition to think well of every body, which is fometimes found in thofe who are juft entering into life, and know not how to fufpect any infincerity in words, or bad defign in actions: this belongs only to youth and inexperience, and therefore cannot laft long in any one. A little knowledge of mankind muft deftroy the pleafing illufion, and fhew a world far different from what the imagination of an innocent and benevolent heart had reprefented it.

Such a difcovery is unavoidable. That there are vices and follies in the world muft be evident to all who are not quite ftrangers to it; and there can be no dependance on a favourable opinion founded on ignorance, and which time muft deftroy. It is when this ignorance is difpelled (as it muft be) that the profpect of the world is opened before us, and opinions are formed upon obfervation; and then the worft parts of it, the confequences attending vice and folly, are in general moft expofed to view, while a greater degree of attention and penetration is neceffary, to difcover the humble excellence, and fecret influence of virtue; to convince us that actions are often far different from what they appear to be, that our judgments of them muft always be uncertain, and that therefore reafon and juftice require us o be very diffident of them; while

                                        candour

candour teaches us to make every allowance which the circumftances of the cafe (according to the beft view we are able to take) can admit; and charity gladly cherifhes the hope that we might find reafon for many more, if we were able to look into the heart.

But while we admire this candid and liberal way of judging, which belongs to an enlarged mind and a benevolent heart, we fhould at the fame time be careful not to confound it with a falfe kind of benevolence, which fometimes affumes the appearance of the true, and tends to produce very pernicious effects. This is, when *faults*, not *perfons*, are made the objects of what is called good-nature; and excufes are found for them, (confidered in themfelves) not for the perfons who are, or appear to be, guilty of them.

To juftify, or even palliate vice, is inconfiftent with truth, and beneath the dignity of virtue; and therefore can never belong to real candour, which is exercifed on the circumftances of the perfon, not on the crime itfelf.

It is by no means improbable, that many may have fallen into errors of this kind with very good intentions, deceived by an appearance of indulgence towards others, which gratifies their good-nature; but fuch fhould remember, that whatever tends to leffen the horror of

vice,

vice, muft be a general injury to all mankind, for which
no advantage to particular perfons can make amends;
and perhaps few are fufficiently fenfible, how greatly
the progrefs of vice is promoted by the foftening terms
fo generally ufed in fpeaking of it, and the favourable
light in which it is fo often reprefented.   By fuch
means the mind by degrees grows familiar with what it
would have confidered as an object of deteftation, had
it been fhewn in its true colours; and none can fay
how far the confequences of this may extend.

Others again are led into this way of judging by their
own intereft, and are glad to find excufes for what
they are confcious of in themfelves, and to fhelter their
felf-indulgence under a pretence of indulgence towards
others.   It is even poffible that they may impofe upon
themfelves, as well as the world, by this method of
proceeding; and may perfuade themfelves that the favourable judgments they pronounce on their neigh-
bours, are really the effects of true benevolence.

Self-indulgence is not the only bad effect which is
likely to follow from hence; for others, who obferve
their fentiments and conduct, and are fenfible of the
bad confequences they are likely to produce, may from
thence be difpofed to run into a contrary extreme, and
to believe that a fuperior regard to virtue is fhewn, by
being

being very fevere in their cenfures upon the conduct of others, and condemning without mercy all thofe who appear to be in any degree blameworthy.

But it fhould always be carefully obferved, as a great and difcriminating character of true candour, by which it may be diftinguifhed from all falfe pretences, that the motives by which it teaches us to be indulgent towards others, are fuch as cannot have that effect when applied to ourfelves, if we fhould ever indulge ourfelves in thofe faults which we condemn in others.

We cannot fee their hearts, and know their motives; and it is very poffible that many an action which is generally condemned, might, if all the circumftances were known, appear to be really deferving of commendation. Perhaps they could explain it, and clear themfelves from the blame thrown on them, but are reftrained from doing it by confideration for others; or fome other good and charitable motive, which makes them willingly fubmit to the cenfure they might avoid, and dare to do right, not only without the fupport of that approbation which fhould be the confequence of it, but even when they know it will expofe them to the contrary.

Perhaps from real and unavoidable ignorance of cir- cumftances which are known to us, they may have

N 3   been

been induced to confider the matter in a very different light, and with very good intentions may have done what appears to us unjuftifiable.

From fuch confiderations as thefe, it will often appear, that what would be a fault in our fituation and circumftances, is really far otherwife in thofe of others, or at leaft may be fo, for ought we can poffibly know to the contrary.

But even where there is no room for any confiderations of this fort, and where we cannot doubt that what we condemn was really a fault, ftill the cafe is widely different between the faults of others and our own. Their error might proceed from ignorance, prejudice, mifapprehenfion, and many other caufes, which he who condemns it can never plead in his own excufe, if he fhould be guilty of the like. They may have been hurried on to act without reflection; but he who obferves and cenfures their conduct, cannot pretend that this is the cafe with him. They may not have been aware of the confequences which would attend their actions; but he who fees them, and condemns the caufe of them, may furely be upon his guard againft it. After the greateft faults, and the longeft deviations from what is right, they may become fenfible of their errors, and reform their lives; but he who dares wilfully

fully to indulge himfelf even in the fmalleft fault, with a view to this, will find his tafk become continually more and more difficult, and has little reafon to expect that he fhall ever accomplifh it.

Thus reafon and juftice teach us to be candid, by fhewing us how very uncertain our judgments on the actions of others muft always be; and how many cir-cumftances, with which we cannot poffibly be fully acquainted, may contribute to alleviate their faults, though they cannot have that effect in regard to our own. They teach us to check that pride which would decide upon every thing, and exalt ourfelves at the expence of others; to be fenfible that there are many things of which we cannot judge; and that the fmalleft deviation from what is right, is inexcufable in our-felves, though the greateft (for ought we know) may admit of many excufes in the cafe of others.

But true charity goes farther ftill. It fhews us in all mankind our brethren and fellow-creatures, for whom we fhould be truly and affectionately interefted. It teaches us to grieve for their faults, as well as for their fufferings; and fincerely and earneftly to wifh their welfare, and endeavour to promote it.

He

He who fees the faults of others with real concern, will not be inclined to aggravate them, nor can he delight to dwell upon them.

He who enjoys all the good he fees, will naturally wifh to fee all in the moft favourable light, and that *wifh* will contribute greatly to enable him to do fo. It will extend even to thofe by whofe faults he is himfelf a fufferer; far from being defirous of revenge, he will grieve for the offender, in this cafe as in every other, and endeavour by the gentleft means to bring him back to what is right.

Our paffions may oppofe what reafon and judgment approve; and, without being able to filence them, may yet often prove too ftrong for them: but that charity which religion infpires, muft be firmly rooted in the heart. It exalts the affections to the higheft object, and fubdues the excefs of paffion by nobler and ftronger inclinations. It extends its influence over the whole character, and is expreffed in the moft trifling converfation as well as in the moft important actions. It is the fource of all thofe difpofitions which are moft amiable and pleafing in fociety, which contribute moft to the happinefs of ourfelves and others here, and which will make us infinitely happy hereafter.

ON THE

ADVANTAGES

OF

AFFLICTION.

IT is the advice of the Wife Man, " In the day of
" adverfity *confider*;" and it may well be reckoned one
of the advantages attending on the afflictions we meet
with in this life, that they call off our attention from
the too eager purfuit of bufinefs or pleafure, and force
us for a time to turn our thoughts another way.
When the difappointment of fome hope we eagerly
purfued, or the lofs of fome bleffing we highly valued,
has deeply impreffed upon our mind the fenfe of our
own weaknefs, and of the uncertainty of every earthly
joy; then furely the importance of fome never-failing
fupport, fome durable felicity, muft ftrike us in the
ftrongeft light. Then, if ever, it behoves us to look
into our hearts, to recall them from thofe tranfitory
pleafures to which they were too much attached, and
endeavour to fix them on hopes which are not liable

to

to difappointment, and joys which nothing in this
world can take away; and to difcover and purfue thofe
means by which we may obtain a rational and well-
grounded enjoyment of fuch hopes, and be prepared
for fuch felicity.

Thofe who enjoy a large portion of the good things
of this life, will often find it very difficult to avoid
growing too much attached to them, and (at leaft in
fome degree) inattentive, perhaps even indifferent, in
regard to another. To fuch, it is evident, the ftroke
which calls them back, however fevere it may be, is
indeed a blefling, if received as it ought to be. But
thofe who are placed in a different fituation, may fometimes ftand no lefs in need of fuch a monitor; their
pleafures being fewer, they may learn to fet a higher
value upon them; and feeling continually the want of
comfort and fupport, they may be apt to reft too much
on fuch as are afforded them, and forget where alone
they muft feek for true and lafting comfort.

Prefent objects make a ftrong impreffion; and even
thofe who appear to have the leaft reafon to be attached
to this world, may yet ftand in need of fome powerful
call to awaken their attention, and raife their thoughts
to a better. But no afflistion can have this effect, if
we immediately fly to pleafure and diffipation, and endeavour

deavour by fuch means to drive it from our thoughts, and render ourfelves infenfible to it. This method may perhaps fucceed in fome degree, or appear to do fo, for a time; but the affliction muft be trifling, or the difpofition little inclined to feel, if fuch methods can deftroy the impreffion it has made. Where the heart has received a real wound, it can never be healed in this way; it will bleed afrefh in every folitary moment, and in fpite of all our endeavours to take off our attention, it will tell us in fecret that this is not the comfort which it wants; and thus the forrow will remain in its full force, but without the advantages which might be derived from it.

If death has fnatched away an affectionate and virtuous friend, how unworthy muft they have been of fuch a bleffing, who can really drive away the remembrance of it, and find comfort for fuch a lofs in the thoughtlefs hurry of trifling amufements? Yet thofe who abandon themfelves to a hopelefs forrow, who cherifh their affliction, and fullenly reject all comfort, will run into an extreme no lefs dangerous, and deftructive of every good and ufeful end which affliction was defigned to anfwer.

Let us then endeavour to feek better refources, and arm ourfelves with more firm and lafting comforts.

Whenever

Whenever it pleafes God to deprive us of a pious
and valuable friend, we may eafily fuppofe it is not
only for the advantage of the deceafed, but for ours
alfo; fince every affliction that happens to us may certainly, if rightly ufed, be conducive to our eternal fal-
vation. Let us humble ourfelves under the afflicting
hand of the Almighty; but let not affliction make us
forget his mercies. Let us thank Him for the bleffings
we have enjoyed; and let us alfo thank Him for making
our afflictions the means of recalling us to Himfelf,
when our affections were too apt to wander from Him,
who is the giver of every good we can enjoy or hope
for. To him let us pour forth all our forrows with
filial confidence, and beg that affiftance and comfort
which can never fail, and will never be denied to thofe
who fincerely feek for them. Let us acknowledge our
own blindnefs and weaknefs, and fincerely refign our
will to his, even in the moft painful facrifices, with the
fulleft conviction, not only of that wifdom and power
which prefide over the univerfe, but alfo of that mercy
and goodnefs by which even the minuteft concerns of
our own lives are directed, and which would permit
no affliction to come upon us but for our greater good.

Let every bleffing we are deprived of in this life ferve
to raife our affections to a better, where all our joys
will be permanent, and eternally fecure; where not only
heavenly

heavenly joys are laid up in ftore for us, but even our deareft earthly treafures will be reftored to us; and where we may hope that we fhall again enjoy them, without any of thofe fears and forrows, thofe weak-neffes and imperfections, which in this life will throw a damp over even our higheft pleafures.

Let us not then endeavour to calm our forrow for our departed friends, by driving them from our remem-brance. To thofe who felt a real and ardent affection, the effort would be vain; nor can we fuppofe it the defign of Providence that we fhould do fo. Such ftrokes are given to force us to reflect: and friends re-moved to a far more exalted ftate, if we think of them as we ought, may be the moft affecting monitors ima-ginable, and their remembrance may prove a moft powerful incitement to every thing that is truly good and worthy.

The opinion that friendfhip lives beyond the grave, is moft foothing to the afflicted mind; and both reafon and fcripture feem to countenance it. The thought that fome fort of intercourfe may be ftill permitted; and that while we continue in this imperfect ftate, it is poffible that they may be allowed to minifter to us for good by means unknown to us, is pleafing; and as we have no affurance of the contrary, it is hardly pof-fible to avoid indulging it.　　　　　　　　This

This indulgence, if kept within due bounds, is furely innocent, and may even be made ufeful to us; but then we fhould remember, that friendfhip in fuch beings muft be free from all thofe weakneffes with which, even in the beft, it will be attended in this imperfect ftate. Though the fame affections may ftill remain, they muft be exalted and refined beyond what we can at prefent form any idea of: they may ftill be watching over us with an affectionate and anxious concern, ftill tenderly folicitous for our real welfare, and rejoicing at every advance we make in piety and goodnefs: but enlightened by a clearer and more extenfive view of things, they can no longer grieve for fufferings which will prove bleffings in the end, or rejoice in profperity, which expofes us to dangerous trials.

Let us confider what fuch a friend would fay, if he could fpeak to us now.——How good, how pious, would he wifh us to be! How trifling would he think the purfuits which are apt to engage fo much of our attention! How powerfully would he preach to us the vanity of all terreftrial enjoyments; and with what ardour would he excite us to exert every faculty of our foul, in endeavouring to fit ourfelves for thofe joys on which time and death can have no power. If he could feel a pain amidft the happinefs in which he is placed, would it not grieve him to fee us indulging our affliction

tion for his lofs, (or any other paffion) fo far as to make us, in any degree, negligent in our duty, and forgetful of that GOD who has beftowed fuch joys on him, and has referved the fame in ftore for us, if we do not forfeit our title to them by our own fault?

If ever we wifhed to give proofs of our affection to our friend, and defire to contribute to his happinefs, let us remember, that the only way in which we can do this, is to live as we are fure he would wifh us to do, if he were ftill a witnefs of our conduct; and for ought we know he may be fo. By thefe means our remembrance of him, far from ftopping us in our courfe, will prove an incitement to every virtue; and the fenfe of prefent forrow will raife the mind to future joy, and add new vigour to all our efforts in the attainment of it.

Fortitude does not confift in being infenfible to the afflictions which come upon us in this world; but he who, when his heart is pierced with forrow, can ftill love his GOD with unabated fervour, and fubmit with entire refignation to his will;—who can ftruggle with his affliction, and refolutely perfift in a conftant endeavour to perform all the duties of his ftation;—that man acts with real fortitude; and when the time fhall come that all his trials are drawing towards a conclufion,

fion; when from the brink of the grave he looks back on the various fcenes of his paft life; thofe feafons of affliction, which once appeared fo fevere, will then be what he can recollect with the greateft fatisfaction; and the remembrance of them will afford him folid confolation, when all the little pleafures of this world are vanifhed and forgotten.

May thefe thoughts be deeply imprinted on my heart! May every affliction be received as it ought to be; and then it will in the end prove a blefling!

PLEASURES

OF

RELIGION.

IN the days of health and eafe, in the hurry of bufinefs and pleafure, our thoughts are often carried away
from thofe objects which ought chiefly to employ
them; and it may require fome effort to call them off
from the pleafing allurements of prefent objects, to
others which appear to be placed at a diftance; though
fuch thoughts might give a far higher relifh to every
innocent pleafure, even at the prefent hour.

Happy indeed are they, whofe prefent pleafures are
fo enjoyed as to be made the means of obtaining everlafting happinefs!—But when a change of circumftances affords more leifure for reflection; when by
ficknefs, affliction, or any other caufe, the pleafures
and purfuits of life are interrupted; thefe excufes can

O

no

no longer be pleaded; and far be it ever from thofe, who by fuch means are in any degree feparated from the world, to judge unfavourably of thofe who are more engaged in it, or value themfelves upon an opinion that they have attained an higher degree of excellence. Their fituations are widely different, and much may be faid to excufe the errors of the thoughtlefs and diffipated, to which the others could have no claim if they fhould ever fall into the like. Let them rather examine the ftate of their own minds, and obferve whether pain does not too often produce the fame bad effect with pleafure; and whether they do not fuffer their thoughts to be too much engaged by prefent evils, inftead of raifing them to what may afford the beft of comforts, and the brighteft hopes.

It feems ftrange that it fhould be difficult to do this; yet all who have been in fuch fituations muft probably at fome time have found it fo, and felt themfelves inclined to dwell on every painful circumftance, though they can only aggravate them by doing fo, and have no temptation of pleafure to plead in their excufe, for they well know that fuch thoughts can only give them pain. But here we alledge, that our thoughts are not under our command;—and it is very certain that they are not entirely fo, efpecially when the fpirits are depreffed, and the mind lefs capable of exertion than at
                                                          other

other times. Yet even on fuch occafions, if fomething we truly valued were propofed as the object of
our purfuit; if we could exprefs our gratitude to fome
kind benefactor, or our affection to fome much-loved
friend; we fhould be difpofed to exert ourfelves, and,
however little our power might be, our thoughts
would be ftill engaged ; we fhould be defirous of doing
all we could, and regret that we could do no more: for
where our affections are truly fixed, our thoughts and
our efforts will be employed.

How many, by fuch confiderations, have been rendered fuperior to fufferings, though not lefs fenfible
of them than others! Something which engages our
affections more ftrongly than prefent eafe or pleafure,
can make us willing to facrifice them; and whatever
could always do that, would be a never-failing fupport
under the lofs of them; and fuch are the comforts
which Religion offers: the love of an All-gracious
Father,—the kindnefs of an Infinite Benefactor,—the
fupport of an Almighty Friend! Here our beft affections may be for ever exercifed, and for ever fatisfied;
and on the exercife of our beft affections, muft all our
happinefs depend : for what is happinefs but the enjoyment of our wifhes; that is to fay, of the objects of
our affections?

O 2   But

But perfect happinefs is not the lot of this life. To be conftantly advancing towards it, continually aiming at it, and continually fuccefsful in that aim, is the utmoft we can hope for here : and this we may enjoy in every fituation of life, when our affections are placed on the Higheft Object: but we can never enjoy it conftantly or fecurely, while they are fixed on any other. Are we afflicted? Our greateft joy remains. Are we difappointed? Our deareft hope cannot be taken away. Are we wounded by unkind-nefs? Our Beft Friend will comfort us. Are we oppreffed by pain and difficulties? Our Almighty Helper will fupport us. Are our good intentions mifreprefented, and our beft actions mifinterpreted? He who fees the heart will do us juftice. Are we neglected and forfaken by the world? He who made and rules the world is ready to receive us, and never will forfake us. Is every forrow heaped upon us, and every earthly comfort fnatched away? The beft of comforts yet remains, and an eternity of happinefs awaits us.

How happy muft be the fituation of a rational creature, exerting all his powers for the beft and nobleft purpofes, performing all the duties of his fta-tion, and making continual advances towards the perfection of his nature; depending with humble confidence

fidence on the divine affiftance to fupport his weaknefs, and conftantly and fincerely endeavouring to do the will of his Heavenly Father; who watches over him with far more than fatherly affection, who orders all events as fhall be really beft for him, accepts his endeavours, forgives his imperfections, and leads him through all the various paths of life to everlafting happinefs!

How delightful is the thought, that we are indeed the objects of HIS love and favour; that all events which can befall us may be made the means of good; that we may flee to HIM as to a tender and faithful friend, in all our forrows, in all our trials, and be certain of that comfort and affiftance of which we ftand in need!

This furely is Happinefs: and this may be enjoyed in every fituation in which we can be placed in this world, for it is totally independent on outward circumftances. All that the world moft values can never beftow it, nor afford true and lafting fatisfaction without it; nor can the greateft afflictions ever take it away. If then, in the time of pleafure and fuccefs, we feel that fomething ftill is wanting to compleat our happinefs, and find our enjoyments difturbed by the dread of lofing them; or if in the time of affliction we

are

are ready to fink beneath our burden; when we are inclined to be diffatisfied or dejected; inftead of giving way to fuch difpofitions, let us think of the happinefs of the ftate we have been defcribing, and afk ourfelves if fuch be really the picture of our fituation? If it be, our pleafures may be enjoyed without anxiety; and in the midft of every trial, we may fay with confidence, " Yet will I rejoice in the Lord, I will joy in " the God of my Salvation;" and fuch joy " no " man taketh from you." Affliction may be felt, human weaknefs may overcloud our joy for a time; but they cannot deftroy it; fuperior to them all, it will conftantly overbalance, and in the end entirely conquer them.

But if this be not our fituation, then let us afk ourfelves why it is not fo? For this happinefs, great as it is, may certainly be attained by all. If then we do not enjoy it, what is the hindrance?—It is vain to plead the weaknefs and imperfection of our nature: for more than is in our power will never be required. By doing the beft we can, we may fecure the favour of our GOD; our weaknefs will be affifted, and our imperfections never laid to our charge.

Does the remembrance of our paft faults deprive us of our happinefs? It need not do fo, fince through

the

the merits of an All-gracious Redeemer, the greateſt will be forgiven, if we repent and forſake them.

Does the ſenſe of our preſent imperfection, and the conſciouſneſs of faults which we frequently fall into, prevent our enjoying it? Let us lay our hand upon our heart, and candidly examine whether it be, or be not, in our power to remedy that imperfection, and avoid thoſe faults? If it be, let us immediately and reſolutely ſet about a work of the utmoſt conſequence to our preſent and future peace;—for certainly, if we can wilfully offend our Maker even in the ſmalleſt inſtance, or neglect any means of expreſſing our love and gratitude to Him, thoſe ſentiments are not felt by us as they ought to be, nor can they produce the hap-pineſs we aim at. If this be not in our power, yet if we really and ſincerely exert our utmoſt endeavours, then what we lament is mere human weakneſs, the the ſenſe of which ſhould never deſtroy our peace; for what we *could not* avoid, will never be imputed as a fault; and involuntary errors and imperfections need not deprive us of our confidence and hope: but then we muſt be ſure that they are involuntary.

And here indeed doubts may ariſe, to which even the beſt muſt often be liable in this imperfect ſtate; for it is by no means ſufficient that we do not offend
deliberately,

deliberately, and with the free confent of the will. If we find ourfelves continually falling into the fame faults, however little they may appear in themfelves, this certainly gives reafon to fufpect fome inclination ftill prevailing in our hearts contrary to that which ought to be the leading principle of every action; and fuch an apprehenfion ought indeed to awaken our attention, and engage us to exert our utmoft diligence to trace the caufe of fuch faults, and fincerely endeavour to root it out, whatever pain the facrifice may coft us: for we fhall by no means form a juft eftimate of our ftate, if we judge of it only from our fentiments in the hours of folitude and reflection. The unguarded moment muft alfo be taken into the account, and may often afford a much clearer infight into the heart, too apt in many ways to impofe upon us, and lead us to form a partial opinion of our own difpofition and conduct.

But though fuch doubts as thefe fhould indeed excite our care and attention, and may often give pain even to thofe whofe intentions are fincerely good, yet ftill they ought not to deftroy their happinefs; for it fhould always be remembered, that the thing required in order to that happinefs is, to do the beft we can, which certainly is always in the power of every one.

This

This confideration can afford no comfort to thofe who knowingly encourage themfelves in any thing wrong, or who neglect to exert their endeavours to conquer their weaknefs, and improve their powers. But it is comfortable indeed to thofe who fincerely wifh and endeavour to do their duty, but who are difcouraged by a fenfe of their imperfections, and difpofed to carry to excefs thofe doubts which in a certain degree are the neceffary confequence of the frailty of human nature, and which are often increafed by difpofitions in themfelves truly laudable; fuch as, humility, caution, an earneft defire of perfection, and very exalted ideas of it. Thofe whofe notions of excellence are not raifed very high, are generally eafily fatisfied with their attainments, and often proud of fuch things as would to others appear fubjects for humiliation and diftruft of themfelves.

The humble and fincere Chriftian may rejoice in the thought, that the enjoyment of the beft of bleffings, the favour of GOD, and everlafting happinefs, is in his power, and never can be forfeited but by his own fault. A diffidence of ourfelves is indeed natural and reafonable, when we reflect on our paft faults, our prefent weaknefs and imperfection, and the exalted purity at which we aim; but this, while it checks every vain and prefumptuous thought, and teaches us
attention

attention and humility, fhould yet never difcourage our hopes, nor deprive us of our peace of mind. It is the fincere endeavour that is required, and will be affifted and accepted, and that is in the power of every one, in every moment of his life. Whatever is paft, he may *now* form a good refolution, exert his efforts, and enjoy the happinefs at which he aims : and this is a happinefs peculiar to Religion alone.

Thofe who fpeak of virtue as its own reward, and dwell on the thought of the heartfelt fatisfaction it muft afford, generally reprefent to their imagination fome exalted inftance of it; they paint to themfelves fome extraordinary exertion of generofity or bene- volence; fome hero who has facrificed every felfifh confideration to the nobleft motives, and exults in the thoughts of his triumph; or fome illuftrious benefac- tor, by whom numbers have been made happy, and who enjoys the happinefs of them all. If they defcend to private life, ftill they take the moment of fome fuc- cefsful exertion of virtue—fome diftrefs relieved, fome good beftowed; fomething, in fhort, which the heart feels, and which the heart, that is not loft to every generous and exalted fentiment, muft feel with delight.

Thefe are pleafures indeed; and thofe who fincerely feek for them, will probably enjoy much more of
                                                              them

them than they might otherwife have imagined; but even fuch will find that many of thefe pleafures are placed beyond their reach, and that they cannot by any be conftantly enjoyed.

To do great actions is the lot of few; and in common life, difappointments often attend the beft endeavours. Poverty, ficknefs, or affliction, check the moft active fpirits, and confine their powers; or even where this is not the cafe, ftill thofe pleafing fuccefsful inftances of virtue muft depend on circumftances which human power is unable to command; and therefore, confidered merely in themfelves, they cannot afford a conftant and never-failing fource of happinefs.

A great part of the lives even of the beft of men muft be fpent in actions which do not afford pleafures of that fort; and though the delight which attends them is certainly a fentiment implanted for wife and gracious purpofes, yet fomething more is neceffary to furnifh a happinefs which may be enjoyed at all times, and in all fituations.

Thofe who have paffed many days, and perhaps years, in conftant and tedious fufferings; who by difeafe, the lofs of any of their faculties, or any other caufe, are rendered a burden to their friends; or perhaps
haps

haps are reduced to a ftate of folitude, and are not fo happy to have any friends about them; whofe utmoft efforts can feldom attain to any thing farther than *leffening* the trouble they muft give to others, and fubmitting with patience to the lot affigned them; fuch perfons will not often find reafon for that exultation of mind, which attends on active and fuccefsful virtue; but on the contrary, finding how little is the utmoft they can do, they will be more inclined to be diffatisfied with themfelves, and hardly able to reconcile themfelves to a life in appearance of fo little ufe.

Thofe who from the unhappinefs of their circumftances and fituations are obliged continually to fuffer from the faults of others; whofe endeavours to pleafe are attended with conftant mortifications and difappointments; and who, by the daily facrifice of their own inclinations, can do nothing more than leffen evils which they are unable to prevent or cure;—far from feeling the triumph of virtue,—will often be obliged to fubmit to the fufferings which fhould attend only on the contrary; and finding their endeavours unfuccefsful, and their conduct frequently blamed, may be led to doubt whether they have not in fome way given occafion to the humiliations which they fuffer; and being unable to fatisfy others, may find it difficult to be fatisfied with themfelves.

Even

Even thofe who are placed in fituations by no means fo painful and difcouraging as thefe, and who meet with much more frequent opportunities of enjoying the fatisfaction of fuccefsful virtue, muft yet fpend a great part of their lives in fuch actions as do not give occafion to it; but which, confidered merely in themfelves, would appear little more than indifferent, and often tedious and infipid.

The little compliances which duty and civility continually require, the employments of domeftic life, and numberlefs other things which muft take up a confiiderable part of the life of every one, and the omiffion of which would be highly improper and even blameable, can yet afford nothing of that heartfelt exultation which is fuppofed to be the attendant of virtue; and which certainly does attend it on many occafions, even where nothing further was confidered than the prefent fatisfaction.

But Religion, by exalting our hopes and efforts to the higheft object, furnifhes a new motive for action, which may extend its influence over every moment of our lives; it teaches us to exalt the moft trifling actions into exertions of virtue; and to find, in the employments of every hour, the means of improvement in thofe heavenly difpofitions which are neceffary to our happinefs both here and hereafter. The

The tedious hours of fuffering afford continual opportunities for the exercife of an affectionate and filial refignation. He who owns a Father's hand in every trial, far from complaining that he is rendered ufelefs to the world, and deprived of the fatisfaction he might have enjoyed in beftowing happinefs, will be convinced that his fituation is fuch as is really beft for him; and fubmitting patiently to all the humiliations which attend it, will find, in every pleafure loft, an occafion to exercife the nobleft fentiments.

Thofe who are difcouraged by mortifications and difappointments, fhould confider for whofe fake they act; and, directing all their efforts to pleafe Him who never will reject them, will feel a ftrength of mind which nothing in this world could infpire; will bear for his fake whatever fufferings they may meet with from others; and refolutely perfevere in the path of duty, though attended with no apparent pleafure or fuccefs. They will look up to heaven with humble, yet cheerful confidence, and remember that their tafk is affigned by Him, who only knows what trials are neceffary to improve and confirm their virtues; and that while they do their beft they are fure to be accepted.

The fame difpofition will extend its influence over all thofe actions which are generally confidered as
matters

matters of indifference, or of fmall importance; things which are performed of courfe, and without any particular fatisfaction, or are omitted without confideration of their confequences. The employments of every day and every hour, which are often more influenced by habit than by reflection, even when they are fuch as ought by no means to be neglected; the duties of our calling; the care of families; the little compliances which are required in fociety; the attentions of civility; every thing, in fhort, which it is right to do even on the moft trifling occafions, fhould be done from the fame principle which infpires the moft exalted inftances of virtue, directed to the fame end, and will then be attended with a fatisfaction of the fame kind.

He who would be ready to refign his life, if his duty required the facrifice, will from the fame motive refign his indulgences, his pleafures, his inclinations, his vanity—every thing great or fmall, which the duty of his fituation, and the prefent time, demand from him; and the dulleft hours he is ever obliged to pafs, will be animated by the fame fpirit which is exerted in the moft pleafing and active virtues. In all he will do his beft, he will endeavour to conform to the will of his Heavenly Father, and exprefs his love and gratitude to Him: and thus, in all, the moft exalted fentiments will

will be exercifed and enjoyed, the nobleft efforts will
be exerted, and the fuccefs be fecure.

If then we find ourfelves weary of the employment
in which we are engaged, or feel the time hang heavy
on our hands; let us confider whether we can employ ourfelves in any thing better?   If we can, let us
embrace the opportunity, and be happy.   If we cannot; if fome dull and tedious way of fpending our
time, or merely patient and filent fuffering, be what
our prefent duty requires, (as muft frequently be the
cafe in the lives of all) then let us confider, that by
fubmitting to it cheerfully, we do the beft we can, and
in fo doing are always certain of the divine favour and
acceptance; the gloom is difpelled, the time which
before appeared almoft a blank in life, now opens a
wide field for the exercife of virtue; its pleafures are
felt, and its hopes enjoyed.

Thus may the humble Chriftian, whofe circumftances and abilities are moft confined, and who has
the feweft opportunities for the exercife of active virtue, ftill enjoy the happinefs which attends it; for to
fuch, *that* happinefs depends not on the fituation in
which he is placed, but on the fentiments of the heart;
he performs the tafk affigned to him, whatever the
tafk may be, with the fame views, and with the fame
alacrity;

alacrity; not repining that he cannot choofe his part, but endeavouring to improve to the utmoft that which is allotted for him, and to cultivate by continual exertion, in every different fituation in life, thofe difpofitions which may recommend him to the favour of his Maker, and fit him for that happinefs which is the object of his hopes.

When by ficknefs, afflictions, or any other caufe, our fpirits are depreffed; when the mortifications of fociety, the difappointment of our purfuits, and the little fatisfaction to be met with in earthly pleafures, incline us to be weary of the world; let us take a view of it in another light, and confider it as what it certainly may be—the road to happinefs, the profpect is changed at once, and the moft painful life appears truly defirable.

We complain of the lofs of fome pleafure which we valued; but if all were taken away, that which alone can make this life truly valuable would yet remain, and we fhould ftill have reafon to receive the gift with thankfulnefs, and purfue our courfe with joy.

Let us but paufe a moment, and confider what it is to be able to fay to ourfelves—" I fhall be happy, per" fectly and unchangeably happy, through eternity!"

P   We

We cannot indeed fay this pofitively while we continue in our ftate of trial, but this we can fay,—" I
" may be fo:—it is in my power to be fo;" not indeed
from a dependance on our own ftrength, or a confidence in our own merits; but the ftrength of Almighty
God is ready to affift our weaknefs,—and the merits
of our bleffed Saviour to atone for our imperfections:—and thefe we may obtain; for of thefe a voice
from heaven affures us, " Afk, and ye fhall receive;
" feek, and ye fhall find."

GRATITUDE.

O F all the fentiments of the heart, there is hardly any which appears to be more natural and univerfal than Gratitude. One might, indeed, be almoft inclined to fuppofe it the effect of inftinct, rather than of reafon, fince we fee fuch ftrong appearances of it, even in brutes. Wherever nature is not perverted, gratitude feems to follow kindnefs, as the effect follows the caufe in any other inftance. But amongft the refinements of polifhed life, the voice of nature is often fuppreffed; and under the fhelter of artificial manners, the felfifh paffions are indulged to excefs.

Politenefs, the expreffion of a delicate mind and a benevolent heart, is taught as an art to difguife the want of thefe qualities; and appearances take the place of realities, till the realities themfelves are neglected, and almoft forgotten. Perhaps if the bufy and the gay had leifure to look into their own hearts, they might

find

find that they poffefs more good qualities than they fufpect themfelves of; but fashion is the general guide; and even follies and vices, if they are fashionable, become objects of vanity, and are affected by those who have no title to them. Yet ftill, in the midft of all the variations of fafhion and prejudice, the efteem due to gratitude is in fome degree preferved, and the want of it is a fault which no one would ever confefs.

A difpofition to pride, to anger, to ambition, to indolence, and many other blameable qualities, may have been acknowledged by many; but none ever confeffed a difpofition to ingratitude, and perhaps none ever was confcious of it: and yet, amongft all the complaints made againft the world by thofe who, being out of humour with themfelves, fancy they have reafon to be fo with every body elfe, there is hardly any one more univerfal than that of the ingratitude they have met with. Nor indeed is the complaint confined to fuch perfons alone; for it muft be owned, that even the benevolent heart will fometimes find but too much reafon for it, and muft feel in fome inftances what it would wifh to conceal from all the world.

But fuch inftances fhould not induce us to pronounce a general cenfure ; and perhaps a more enlarged view of mankind might fhew us, that the effects

afcribed

afcribed to ingratitude are often owing to fome other
caufe, and that thofe who make the greateft complaints
are in fact thofe who have the leaft reafon for them,
and have themfelves given occafion to that ingratitude
of which they complain, by expecting fuch returns as
they have no right to claim.

Perhaps thefe complaints, in many inftances, may
be owing to the want of diftinguifhing fufficiently between that fort of gratitude which is paid as a debt,
and that which is a fentiment of the heart. Every
benefit conferred, according to its different degree,
has a right to claim the firft; a word or a look may
infpire the laft more than the gift of millions could
have done.

Thefe two kinds of gratitude are different in many
inftances, and may be entirely feparated; but painful
indeed is the lot of him who is reduced to *owe* the firft,
where he is unable to *feel* the laft: for the firft alone
may be indeed a burden,—the laft is always a pleafure;
the firft would be glad to return more than it has received, by way of difcharging the debt,—the laft would
make every return in its power, by way of exprefling
what it feels, but would never wifh to lofe the impreffion. In fhort, the one is the return due to *benefits*,
the other to *kindnefs*; the one may be claimed, and

P 3   muft

muſt be paid; but even to mention a *claim* to the other, would endanger the title to it.

That benefits alone cannot give a right to this ſort of gratitude, will be evident, if we conſider that it is a ſentiment of the heart, which is, and can be paid only to kindneſs, or the appearance of kindneſs; and benefits may ſpring from very different motives, in which perhaps the perſon on whom they are conferred has in reality no concern, nor ever was the object in view; they may be embittered by a thouſand circumſtances which may make it a pain to receive them; or even without theſe, they may want that kindneſs which alone can make it a pleaſure to a delicate mind.

In the early part of life, when the ſentiments have generally more vivacity than refinement, and before experience has taught the fatal art of allaying every pleaſure by ſuſpicion, theſe two kinds of gratitude generally go together. Every benefit is ſuppoſed to proceed from kindneſs, and is felt as ſuch; and as all the benevolent affections of an innocent heart are attended with pleaſure, they are generally at that time carried almoſt to exceſs. Every appearance of kindneſs is then received with warm and affectionate gratitude. Imagination beſtows a thouſand excellencies on the perſon from whom it comes; every thing is expected from the ſuppoſed

pofed friend, and every expreffion of gratitude feems
too little to return the kindnefs received. Perhaps a
little time difcovers the deceit; the obligation is found
to have proceeded from fome motive quite different
from what was imagined; and the perfon who conferred it finks to a level with the reft of the world, and
difappoints all the hopes which had been formed. The
affectionate and grateful heart remains the fame as before; but the object to which that affection and gratitude were addreffed, is no longer to be found; it wifhes
to preferve the fame fentiments, and grieves that it is
unable to feel them: but the apparent change proceeds
only from the former miftakes. Probably there is
hardly any perfon of ftrong fenfibility who has not experienced mortifications of this fort; and ingratitude
may often have been laid to the charge of thofe, whofe
only fault was, that they carried their gratitude, and
their expreffions of it, to excefs, without fufficiently
confidering what grounds they had for it. Thofe who
make the complaint might by a different conduct have
preferved their claim, but complaints can never regain
what they have loft; to expect it, would be to fuppofe
that unkindnefs fhould produce the fame effect as
kindnefs.

Far be it ever from our thoughts to offer any excufe
for real ingratitude. The perfon who is capable of it

is

is a monfter in nature, whom all agree to condemn, and all would wifh to avoid.   But the greater our horror of the crime, the greater fhould be our caution not to charge any with it unjuftly; and greater care and attention are neceffary never to give occafion to it.

Thofe who are fo ready to complain of the want of gratitude in others, fhould examine their own hearts, and enquire whether they really have any right to that return which they expect;—whether true kindnefs was indeed their motive;—and whether they have not allayed the obligation by fuch circumftances as muft deftroy the effect of it, and leave no impreffion but a painful confcioufnefs of owing a debt, inftead of that heartfelt gratitude which enjoys the thought of it? While thofe who wifh to infpire true gratitude, fhould confider the means by which it may be gained; and they are fuch as, more or lefs, are generally in the power of all.

To beftow confiderable benefits, belongs indeed to few; but that kindnefs which comes from the heart, and which the heart feels and returns, is totally independent on fuch circumftances.   Without this, the greateft benefits may give pain; with it, a trifle becomes important, and infpires true and lafting gratitude.   For the exercife of this, numberlefs opportunities are continually

tinually prefenting themfelves in the daily intercourfe of life; and thofe who are attentive to take advantage of them, will hardly be wanting on greater occafions, either in doing acts of kindnefs, or in that manner of doing them, which changes an obligation from a burden to a pleafure. They can enter into the feelings of thofe they oblige, and are eager to fpare them every circumftance which may be painful; while thofe who act upon different motives, will expect more than they have any title to, and probably much more than they themfelves would pay, if they could change places with the perfons obliged; for the exclufive regard to *felf*, which makes them complain fo loudly of the ingratitude they have met with, would probably make them ungrateful in their turn, if they were to receive obligations inftead of conferring them.

But while we are confidering that benevolence of heart which fhould be the fource of every act of kindnefs, and that delicacy of manners with which all fuch acts fhould be attended, (and indeed it is impoffible to confider them in too ftrong a light) let us not however forget, that the want of thefe can by no means difcharge the perfon obliged from gratitude confidered as a *duty*; that is to fay, from as much as it is in his power to pay; for more than that can never be required.

Monfieur

Monfieur Du Clos, in his ingenious and elegant effay, " *Sur les Mœurs*," has many excellent reflections on this fubject, in which the duties of perfons obliged are confidered at large: (fee chap. 16. *fur la Reconnoiffance*, & *fur l'Ingratitude*.) He concludes with an obfervation well deferving particular attention, becaufe it fets in a ftrong light the fallacy of an opinion which, like many others, has been too generally received without fufficient examination, merely becaufe it founds plaufible. His words are thefe:—

" J'ai plufieurs fois entendu avancer fur ce fujet
" une opinion qui ne me paroit ni jufte ni decente.
" Le caractere vindicatif part, dit-on, du même prin-
" cipe que le caractere reconnoiffant, parcequ'il eft
" également naturel de fe fouvenir des bons & des
" mauvais fervices. Si le fimple fouvenir du bien et
" du mal qu'on a eprouvé etoit la regle du reffenti-
" ment qu'on en garde, on auroit raifon; mais il n'y
" a rien de fi different, ni même de fi peu dependant
" l'un de l'autre. L'efprit vindicatif part de l'orgueil,
" fouvent uni avec le fentiment de fa propre foibleffe;
" on s'eftime trop, et l'on craint beaucoup. La recon-
" noiffance marque d'abord un efprit de juftice, mais
" elle fuppofe encore une ame difpofée à aimer, pour
" qui la haine feroit un tourment, et qui s'en affran-
" chit plus encore par fentiment que par reflexion. Il
" y a

" y a certainement des caracteres plus aimants que
" d'autres, et ceux-la font reconnoiffans par le principe
" même qui les empeche d'être vindicatifs."

This fuppofed connection between certain good and
bad qualities, is an opinion we find often maintained,
without being fufficiently examined; though probably,
in moft inftances, it would be found directly contrary
to the truth, as it has been fhewn to be in this; and
the confequences of fuch an opinion are often of much
greater importance than may at firft be imagined.

Pride, for inftance, is generally faid to attend on fuperior talents and attainments. In confequence of this
opinion, how often do we fee thofe who are deftitute of
both, affecting that vanity which they fuppofe to belong to them, and endeavouring to gain the reputation
of fuperior excellence, by affuming the appearance of
the fault which they imagine is connected with it;
while thofe who poffefs the qualities which others
would affect, are continually afpiring to greater degrees of excellence; and finding that their higheft attainments always fall fhort of their wifhes, even by
thofe attainments are taught humility.

The fame might be obferved in many other inftances. Virtue and vice, the amiable and unamiable
qualities,

qualities, are in their own nature oppofite, and more
or lefs tend to deftroy each other, whenever they fubfift in any degree in the fame charaćter; and perhaps
the moft effećtual way of eradicating any bad difpofition from the minds of young perfons, is not fo much
by attacking it directly, as by endeavouring to cultivate
thofe good qualities which are particularly contrary to
it, and to give them a clear and juft idea of thofe
which they may have been led to imagine are connećted
with it.

To the truly affećtionate and grateful heart, every
opportunity of exercifing thofe qualities affords real
enjoyment: it cannot help feeking out for them, becaufe from thofe feelings it muft derive its greateft
pleafures; without the exercife of them, it cannot be
happy.   How then can it be fo in exercifing fuch as are
contrary to them? A very little reafoning and reflection muft furely be fufficient to convince any one of
the fallacy of fuch an opinion; but to thofe who really
feel that difpofition to affećtion and gratitude of which
others *talk*, all reafoning upon the fubjećt muft be unneceffary: thofe fentiments will be ever cherifhed; and
notwithftanding the many mortifications and difappointments with which they may be attended, they
will ftill, in fome degree, carry their reward along with
them.   Our feelings are greatly influenced by our
                                           purfuits,

purfuits, and by thofe objects which engage our at- .
tention. The perfon who is continually in purfuit of
opportunities for exercifing the benevolent affections,
either by conferring or acknowledging kindnefs, will
overlook a thoufand trifling caufes of offence which
might have awakened refentment in the breaft of another; while thofe in whom the felfifh paffions prevail,
will be equally infenfible to numberlefs inftances of
kindnefs, which would have filled the hearts of others
with gratitude and joy; juft as a perfon who is eager in
the chace will difregard the beauties of the profpect
which furrounds him, and know no more of the country
through which he paffed than if he never had feen it.

But while the affectionate and grateful heart thus
purfues and enjoys every opportunity of exercifing thofe
qualities, it muft be owned at the fame time, that they
may lead to many mortifications and difappointments.
Thofe who are eager to catch at every appearance of
kindnefs may fometimes be mifled by falfe appearances;
and thofe who are difpofed to love all who have fhewn
them any kindnefs, may afterwards find that their affection has been mifplaced.

To prevent fuch miftakes, as far as the obfervation
of mankind and delicacy of judgment can do it, is certainly defirable; but to avoid them entirely, is perhaps
impoffible:

impoſſible: and ſurely none would wiſh to avoid them by running into the contrary extreme, and loſing all the pleaſures attending on ſuch diſpoſitions.

It ſhould however be obſerved, that this diſpoſition to ſeek for obligations relates to kindneſſes, rather than to conſiderable benefits. Affection muſt precede the benefit, or at leaſt muſt be engaged by the manner of conferring it, in order to make it a pleaſure to a perſon of true delicacy. This does not proceed from pride; but becauſe ſuch a perſon, having a high ſenſe of gratitude, is unwilling to contract an engagement to one he cannot eſteem and love. To be unable to entertain thoſe ſentiments which might be thought due, would be to him a continual ſuffering; while one whoſe feelings are centered in himſelf, is glad to get what he wants at any rate, and gives himſelf no concern about making any return for it; or at leaſt thinks he has done this very ſufficiently by conferring ſome favour which he imagines to be equivalent to what he has received. Yet, in fact, a real obligation freely conferred on one who had no claim to it, and willingly received by him as ſuch, can never afterwards be cancelled by any act of the perſon who received it, even though it ſhould be in his power to return benefits far beyond what he has received; becauſe, in one reſpect, they muſt always fall ſhort of it: for the firſt benefit conferred was a free and

and unmerited kindnefs, to which the perfon obliged
had no title; but no return can ever be fuch; and all
that can be done in confequence of it, is ftill but a *return*, however it may exceed in other refpects; fo that
the perfon who once acknowledges himfelf to be under
an obligation, though he may not be bound to make
all the returns which an unreafonable perfon may require, is yet bound for ever to acknowledge it.

This however relates chiefly to fuch obligations as
are really conferred with a view to ferve the perfon obliged.   The cafe is different when one perfon is benefited by another merely from a concurrence of accidental
circumftances, or when the benefit was conferred from
oftentation, or with a view to gain fome greater benefit
in return.   In thefe laft cafes indeed it feems a fort of
bargain, in which the perfon who gains what he aimed
at, has received his price, and has no reafon to complain.   Yet even in thefe, and indeed in every inftance,
the truly grateful will ever be ready to acknowledge the
obligations received, in their various degrees, though
the fentiments excited by fuch obligations are far different from thofe which are the return due to real
kindnefs.

That gratitude may fometimes be a duty when it is
not a pleafure, is but too certain; that from being a
                                                   true

true and heartfelt pleasure, it may become a burden, is no less so; but the pleasure of self-approbation still remains to compensate these mortifications: and they must be insensible indeed, who ever felt that pleasure while they were acting an ungrateful part, or who can be happy without feeling it.

The proud and selfish generally mistake their own happiness, and in no instance more than in this of gratitude. Those who know what it is to feel its tenderest and most refined sentiments, when the kindness of some friend, truly loved and valued, makes the heart overflow with gratitude and joy, and all language seems too weak to express what it feels, will be little inclined to envy those who are too proud to be obliged, and too self-sufficient to think they stand in need of any thing which the kindness of others can bestow. Even the little acts of kindness attending on the daily occurrences of life, afford pleasure far beyond *their* reach; for the intercourse of real kindness, and that gratitude which is its due return, whether expressed in the smallest or the greatest matters, is always attended with a heartfelt satisfaction on both sides; and they know little of their own interest, who from pride, insensibility, or inattention, neglect the opportunities, which, in a greater or less degree, are continually offering themselves for enjoying it.

But

But if the grateful heart experience such satisfaction in the sentiments excited by little and imperfect kindnesses, and paid to frail and imperfect beings, how exquisite must be the delight attending on that gratitude which is excited by Infinite Obligations, and paid to Infinite Perfection! No doubt can here intervene as to the motive which gave occasion to the benefit conferred. We had no claim on our Almighty Benefactor, and can make him no return: for we have nothing but what we have received. Here we can have no apprehension of carrying our love and gratitude too far, and being reduced to grieve for the faults and imperfections of those on whom they were bestowed, and from whom they cannot now be recalled. All is perfection of goodness, and all our love and gratitude must ever fall short of what we owe. No fears can here arise of a change of conduct, or that a friend and benefactor may cease to be such, and wound the grateful heart by unkindnefs and upbraidings; the same goodness will for ever continue, and our warmest gratitude be ever overpaid by new instances of that kindnefs which can never fail but through our own fault.

Religion to the truly grateful heart is a continual exercise of that virtue; and considered in this view, what a pleafure is diffused over the most painful trials to which it can ever call us!——

Q   Our

Our exiſtence, with every bleſſing attending on it;
—our redemption, with the hopes of peace and pardon
ſecured by it;—and an eternity of happineſs prepared
for us hereafter;—are ſurely benefits ſufficient to
awaken gratitude in the moſt unfeeling heart: and can
it be poſſible that thoſe on whom a kind word or look
can make an impreſſion never to be effaced, ſhould be
infenſible to benefits like theſe, or return them merely
by a cold obedience, often paid unwillingly, inſtead of
that warm and animated gratitude, which thinks it can
never do enough to expreſs what it feels?

Gratitude excited by real kindneſs, and joined with
true affection and eſteem, can never be a lifeleſs, inactive ſentiment; it will be continually ſeeking opportunities to expreſs itſelf; it will conſider every ſuch
opportunity as a valuable acquiſition; and though it
ſhould be attended with pain and difficulty, it will find
a ſatisfaction even in theſe, becauſe in theſe it can ſhew
itſelf moſt ſtrongly. It will exert itſelf even in trifles,
and be expreſſed in words and looks, though nothing
farther ſhould be in its power.

But when gratitude is raiſed to the Higheſt Object,
the means of expreſſing it can never be wanting; every
exerciſe of every virtue performed with that view will
be accepted as ſuch; and what a ſatisfaction muſt the
grateful

grateful heart enjoy, from the thought of being continually employed in exprefling its fentiments, by making fuch returns as the Almighty Benefactor requires, and will accept!

With this view, how earneftly will it feek for every means of doing good to others! With what patience and benevolence will it fupport every injury received, and endeavour by the gentleft means to bring back offenders to peace and goodnefs, inftead of exafperating them by reproaches and upbraidings!

Confidered in this view, how pleafing will every difficult exercife of virtue appear; and what a never-failing fource of comfort and fatisfaction will be found even in the fevereft fufferings to which human nature is liable! All may ferve to exprefs our gratitude; and to thofe who truly feel it, this muft always be a pleafure. Nor need the meaneft and the weakeft ever be afraid that their humble efforts will pafs unnoticed. Earthly benefactors may be removed beyond our reach; and even when prefent, they are liable to be mifled by falfe appearances, and may be often miftaken in the opinions they form of the gratitude they have met with; but He who fees the heart, will obferve and accept the filent wifhes of the truly grateful, when wifhes only are in their power, for it is the gratitude

Q 2   of

of the heart which He requires; the means of expref-
ing it depend on outward circumftances.

How happy then are they in whom thefe fentiments
are warm and active!—for here gratitude is continually
excited by new benefits; and here it may be indulged
to the greateft height, without fear of excefs, and without doubt of acceptance.   The heavenly intercourfe is
continued through life.   Religion, inftead of being a
reftraint upon the inclinations, becomes an indulgence
of them.   Numberlefs inftances of infinite goodnefs
are difcovered, which would efcape the obfervation of
the thoughtlefs and inattentive.   The pleafure of gratitude is increafed by every exercife of it; and new
efforts are continually excited to make every poffible
return; efforts which muft always be attended with a
heartfelt pleafure, becaufe they flow from a delightful
principle, and are certain of fuccefs.

Thus may gratitude afford continual pleafures even
in this world, and lead us at length to that bleffed ftate,
where it will be continually excited by unbounded
benefits, and exercifed and enjoyed through eternity.

ON

HAPPINESS.

WHOEVER takes an attentive survey of mankind, cannot fail to be struck with this observation—That, in general, all are roving about in pursuit of enjoyment, and seldom think of seeking it within themselves.

It is very certain that man was formed for society; and it is his duty, as well as interest, to cultivate a social disposition; to endeavour to make himself useful and pleasing to others; to promote and to enjoy their happiness; to encourage the friendly affections, and find in them the source of the greatest pleasures which this world can bestow. But, alas! Society too often exhibits a far different scene. We see weariness and disgust reign in the gayest assemblies.

Conversation, instead of turning upon such subjects as might at once afford amusement and improvement,

Q 3   often

often languishes for want of materials, or is engrossed by
the most trifling subjects, so that it is often merely an
idle dissipation of time—perhaps even a pernicious
abuse of it; since it may afford opportunities for the
exercise of many bad qualities, which, by appearing in
disguise, are rendered still more mischievous. Ill-nature
shelters itself under the mask of wit. A desire to de-
preciate the merit of the absent, or perhaps to mortify
the present, endeavours to pass itself off for the love of
sincerity and truth, or for a superior degree of zeal in
the cause of virtue. Vanity assumes the appearance of
every good and amiable quality, as occasion offers; or
flatters the weaknesses of others, and applauds what
ought to be condemned, in hopes of gaining favour, and
being flattered in return. Sometimes merely for want
of something to say, and without the least intention of
doing mischief, an idle report is repeated, which tends
to injure an innocent person—perhaps irreparably; or
fix a trifling ridicule upon a worthy character, and
thereby destroy the influence of its good example.
By these, and numberless other means, conversation is
perverted from that purpose for which it was intended;
and a meeting of rational beings, which should have
contributed to improve the powers of their minds, by
mutually assisting each other, and to strengthen the ties
of affection and benevolence, by the continual exercise
of those qualities, often produces a quite contrary effect;

and

and they part, filled with far different fentiments, and weary and diffatisfied with themfelves and with each other.

Many caufes might be affigned for this ftrange, though too frequent abufe of what feems calculated to afford the higheft rational entertainment, fince every vice and folly contributes towards it; but amongft others, this is certainly one—That mankind often feek fociety, not with a view to be ufeful and pleafing to others, or even with any great expectation of being pleafed themfelves, but merely becaufe they know not how to amufe themfelves alone; and thofe who affociate with others, becaufe they are weary of themfelves, are not very likely to contribute to the pleafure or advantage of fociety.

While all are in purfuit of happinefs, it is ftrange to obferve, that there are fo few who cultivate and improve thofe powers which they poffefs within themfelves; and the confequences of this neglect are certainly much more fatal, even to prefent happinefs, than is generally imagined.

Suppofing it were poffible, that thofe who cannot pleafe themfelves in folitude fhould be able to pleafe others, and be happy in fociety; yet it is impoffible to

be

be always engaged in it: and even thofe who have
the greateft opportunities of enjoying it, know not how
foon they may be reduced to a ftate of folitude. It is
therefore highly neceffary for all, to provide themfelves
with folitary pleafures; for the mind of man is naturally active; it wants employment and amufement,
and if it be not fupplied with fuch as are innocent and
ufeful, it will be apt to fink into a ftate of languor and
difguft, or run aftray into the wildeft extravagancies of
fancy, which may lead infenfibly into endlefs doubts
and errors, productive of confequences which may
prove fatal to happinefs both here and hereafter.

It is therefore certainly a point of importance to all,
and efpecially to thofe who are entering into life, to cultivate thofe powers and difpofitions of mind which may
prove fources of innocent amufement. When thefe
are neglected, they are eafily loft; but being exercifed,
they will continually improve; and if properly directed,
they may be productive of much advantage as well
as pleafure.

The impreffion which any object makes upon the
mind, often depends much lefs upon the object itfelf,
than on the difpofition of the perfon who receives it,
and the light in which he has been accuftomed to confider things.

Suppofe

Suppofe a large number of perfons entering at once into a thick wood:—One will enjoy the refrefhing fhade; another will complain that it deprives him of the profpect; a third will be employed in obferving the various kinds of trees and plants which it contains; a fourth will confider them as the riches of the nation, he will form them in imagination into fhips, and fuppofe them maintaining the empire of the feas, or fpreading our commerce round the world; another will think of the money they might produce, he will long for the power of levelling them all with the ground, and carrying the profits to the gaming-table:—perhaps to fome it may appear only as a gloomy folitude, which they wifh to quit as foon as poffible; while others, ftruck with the awful fcenery of the place, feel their minds elevated by it, and enjoy an exalted kind of pleafure, which can only be felt, but never can be defcribed. Others again confider it merely as the path they muft pafs through, and go on as faft as they can, without paying the leaft attention to the objects which furround them. Yet the foreft is ftill the fame, and as an object of fenfe makes the fame impreffion on all; though the emotions excited in the mind may perhaps be different in every one who enters it.

The fame will be found to be the cafe in regard to moft of the objects which engage our attention; and though

though this difference in the impreffion made by them, depends in fome degree on natural difpofition, yet certainly it alfo depends on many circumftances which are by no means as independent on ourfelves as we are apt to imagine.

One perfon takes a book merely to pafs away the time: another takes it in hopes of gaining admiration afterwards, by difplaying the knowledge he has acquired:—the firft is tired, the fecond difappointed; yet perhaps the book was calculated to yield both pleafure and improvement to one who read it with a view to thefe.

Another reads becaufe it is the fafhion, and thinks to acquire the reputation of tafte, by admiring what has been admired by thofe who are efteemed good judges; but his reading muft be a tafk, fince his memory, not his feelings and his judgment, muft inform him when he is to be pleafed, and what he is to commend.

Another takes a contrary method, and thinks he fhall fhew fuperior delicacy and penetration by difliking what others approve, and difcovering faults which they did not obferve: he reads with a refolution not to be pleafed, and in this he will certainly fucceed; and will not only deprive himfelf of a prefent pleafure, but the fame difpofition will probably be extended to other inftances,

ftances, and by degrees may poifon all the fweets of
life; for every pleafure in this world muft in its own
nature be imperfect; and thofe who accuftom themfelves to feek for fomething to find fault with, will acquire an habit of viewing the dark fide of every thing,
till they lofe the power of enjoying any pleafure, and
the whole world can afford them nothing but objects
of diflike.

We may be amufed for a time with what only ftrikes
the fenfes, or engages the attention. A fine picture, a
beautiful profpect, a melodious voice, an entertaining
hiftory, can hardly fail to afford fome pleafure to every
one; but they will make a flight impreffion on thofe
who have never cultivated a tafte for fuch things; for
any pleafure in which the mind is merely paffive, can
afford only a tranfient fatisfaction; but when the object
prefented to us (of whatever kind it may be) awakens
the imagination, and calls the powers of the mind into
action, it may then be really enjoyed, and may lead to
pleafures far beyond what at firft fight it feemed calculated to produce, by exciting new fentiments and reflections, and exercifing and improving thofe faculties
on which our enjoyments fo much depend.

There is a certain indolence of mind in many perfons, which is no lefs prejudicial to their happinefs than

to

to their improvement: they will not be at the trouble
of seeking for pleasures in their own stores, or of contributing their part to the enjoyment of those which
are presented to them, but run continually from one
object to another, and spend their lives in a fruitless
pursuit of what, by the help of a little exertion, they
might have found in numberless instances which they
have overlooked; and what, in fact, they never can
enjoy, while they consider it as totally independent on
themselves.

It is owing to this that we see all places of public
amusement so much frequented by persons who appear to take no pleasure in them.   They cannot amuse
themselves, and therefore they go where they are told
amusement will be provided for them; and though
they feel themselves disappointed, they are unwilling to
own it either to themselves or others, for they know
no remedy, nor will they be at the trouble of seeking
any.   This gives an air of gloominess to every place
of amusement, for even the gayest scenes cannot afford
pleasure to those who do not bring with them a disposition to be pleased themselves, and to enjoy and endeavour to promote the pleasure of others.

It has been observed, that pain would be a trifle,
could we banish memory and anticipation, and feel
only

only that of the prefent moment: the fame will be found true in regard to pleafure. We muft reflect, in order to fuffer or enjoy in any great degree. The pleafure which drives away thought will be felt only for the moment, and will leave a vacancy of mind behind it, which will foon lead to that ftate of diftafte and wearinefs fo contrary to every real enjoyment, and often more difficult to fupport than even pofitive fufferings.

This is true, not only of trifling amufements, but even of thofe of a more exalted kind. Reflection is neceffary to the enjoyment of all; and therefore to acquire an habit of it, is a point of the utmoft importance to happinefs in every fituation in life; yet it is a point much too little attended to, in moft fyftems of education.

Inftruction (according to the ufual method) confifts in exercifing the memory, while the other powers of the mind are neglected, and either become totally inactive, or elfe run wild into a thoufand extravagancies, and prove the moft fatal enemies to that happinefs which they were intended to promote; in order to which, it is neceffary that they fhould be cultivated and improved, and directed to proper objects, not loft for want of exertion, nor fuppreffed from a fear of the mifchiefs they may occafion.

The

The beft book, or the moft inftructive converfation, will afford little pleafure or advantage, by being merely remembered, in comparifon of what it might afford by exciting new reflections in the mind, which lead to a new train of thought, and make the riches of others become in fome fort its own. Without this, every kind of ftudy will be dull and uninterefting, becaufe it will only fill the memory, without improving the mind, or affecting the heart.

A new language will only furnifh a new fet of words; but by comparing it with thofe already known, we might find means of explaining our fentiments and ideas more diftinctly, and perhaps of fetting things in a clearer light, even to ourfelves.

The ftudy of any branch of philofophy, inftead of being merely an employment for the memory, may tend to new obfervations and difcoveries, and raife the mind by degrees to contemplations of a far higher kind.

Hiftory, inftead of fupplying us only with the know-ledge of facts, may give us a farther infight into the human heart, and furnifh many ufeful obfervations in regard to our conduct in life, if we accuftom ourfelves to feek the remote caufes of great events, and trace to their fource the fecret fprings of action, which will often be

be found far different from what at firſt ſight they appear to have been.

Poetry, from a trifling amuſement, may be raiſed to
a pleaſure of the higheſt kind, if it makes us feel more
ſtrongly the exalted ſentiments which it expreſſes, and
elevates the mind to a contemplation of its native dignity, and a conſciouſneſs of powers for enjoyment beyond what any thing in this world can ſatisfy.

By ſuch methods as theſe, ſome kind of improvement may be found in almoſt every ſtudy, beſides that
which is its immediate object; and a conſciouſneſs of
improvement is a never-failing ſource of pleaſure.

The ſame method might alſo often be applied to the
common occurrences of private life. Whenever improvement is really the object of purſuit, numberleſs
opportunities for attaining it (too generally overlooked)
will be continually preſenting themſelves; and it is
aſtoniſhing to obſerve how often ſuch opportunities are
loſt, from mere inattention, and for want of being accuſtomed to look within ourſelves. Thoſe who are
continually employed in endeavouring to diſplay their
talents to others, will ſcarce ever do this to any pur-
poſe; their attention is engaged by what they wiſh to
appear to be, not by what they really are: and this is
                                                    often

often carried fo far, that they impofe upon themfelves
as well as others; and while this deception continues
the evil is without a remedy, and all hope of improvement muft be entirely at a ftand.

There is indeed hardly any thing fo fatal to improvement of every kind, as the practice which too generally
prevails in the world, of fubftituting appearances in the
place of realities; and thofe inftructions which teach
the art of doing this (however plaufible they may appear in many inftances) will be found to be far more
pernicious than at firft fight would be imagined, not
only by fetting up another object of purfuit, in the place
of real improvement, and teaching a continual habit of
deceit, but alfo by bringing true merit into difcredit.
Thofe who are confcious that they are acting a part
themfelves, will always be apt to fufpect others of doing
the like; and thofe who can find means of acquiring
the reputation of merit of any kind, which they do not
poffefs, will hardly be at the trouble afterwards of endeavouring to acquire the reality.

In folitude, there is much lefs danger of felf-deceit.
Our thoughts are not diffipated by a variety of objects,
nor employed in endeavouring to gain the good opinion
of others; nor is the judgment we form of ourfelves
made dependent on that opinion, as it fometimes happens

pens in fociety, efpecially when we have any reafon to believe that it inclines to the fide moft favourable to our vanity. We muft then feel and improve thofe powers which we poffefs, in order to enjoy them; and for this reafon, as well as many others, it may be highly ufeful to all, to be fometimes accuftomed to folitude; efpecially in the early part of life, while the mind enjoys its full vigour, and the fpirits are not broken by ficknefs and afflictions; they will then find the refources which they poffefs, and learn that it is poffible to amufe and improve themfelves.

Probably a time will come when folitude will be unavoidable, or when, from diftafte to fociety or many other caufes, it may appear defirable. But to thofe who have never been accuftomed to enjoy the pleafures and advantages it might afford, it will then (in all probability) be a painful and dangerous fituation. Unconfcious of thofe refources which they might have found within themfelves, and unaccuftomed to intellectual pleafures, they will hardly be able to acquire a relifh for them at a time when the fpirits, and perhaps the temper, are impaired by the difappointments and mortifications of fociety. They will be apt to dwell on difcontented thoughts, and fancy themfelves better than the reft of the world, merely becaufe they are weary of it, till their benevolence is weakened by con-

R tinually

tinually viewing every thing in the worft light, and they grow proud of the faults of others, not of their own good qualities.

In fuch a ftate of mind, no advantage will be gained by being obliged to take a nearer view of their own character and conduct; for inftead of comparing themfelves with that degree of excellence which they might have attained, they will form their judgment by a comparifon of themfelves with the unfavourable opinion they have formed of others; and their ill-humour, as well as their vanity, will fecure to themfelves the preference, yet will deprive them at the fame time of any fatisfaction this preference might afford; for their ill-humour will make them a burden to themfelves, and their vanity will make them eager to gain the applaufe of others, and be continually mortified and difappointed at finding they do not fucceed. Thus the gloom of folitude will be added to the difgufts of fociety; the pleafures of the one will be loft, and thofe of the other unknown or unenjoyed.

It is impoffible to enumerate the pleafures which a thinking mind may find within itfelf, or the advantages which may be derived from them; they are far beyond all defcription, and can only be known by being enjoyed. Indeed from a difference of character and circumftances,

they

they may perhaps be different in every perfon; but every one who feeks them, will probably find that he may enjoy much more than he had any notion of.

How delightful might it be to trace to ourfelves the image of all that is moft beautiful and pleafing in nature, to renew the impreffion which fuch objects have formerly made upon the mind, and then endeavour to improve in imagination upon what we have feen;—to obferve the caufes of thofe effects which we fee, as far as they are obvious to our notice, and try to difcover thofe which are yet unknown to us;—to recal fuch paft events as have afforded us true pleafure, and to anticipate fuch as we may hereafter hope for, or paint to ourfelves fcenes more pleafing than any we have ever yet known, or probably fhall ever find in this world;—to foar beyond all bounds of fpace or time, and try to catch a glance at objects which are far beyond our prefent powers of comprehenfion;—in fhort, to exert the powers of the mind, to enjoy and improve thofe faculties by which man is diftinguifhed from the inferior creation; to feel that they are independent on outward objects, and rejoice in the confcioufnefs of the dignity of our nature!

Every amiable quality and difpofition of the heart, all that is good and pleafing in fociety, may alfo, in a

R 2   certain

certain degree, be exercifed in imagination, and cultivated and enjoyed in folitude.

Our gratitude may be employed, in recollecting the
kindneffes we have received; we may ftill dwell with
pleafure on the fentiments they excite, though deprived of the power of expreffing them.

Our humility may be exercifed, by taking a nearer
view of our own imperfections, undifguifed by that
falfe colouring which our paffions are apt to throw
over them, while we are engaged in fociety; yet at the
fame time, the fenfe of our own weaknefs teaches us
to be more indulgent to that of others.

Our candour may be employed, in driving away the
prejudices through which we are apt to view their
words and actions, when they happen to wound our
pride, or oppofe our purfuits. While we feel ourfelves hurt, we are apt to aggravate the fault of the
offender, which perhaps, if confidered in its true light,
and afcribed to its true motives, would appear to be
no fault at all.

Our benevolence may be exerted, in contriving
fchemes to do good to others, which, even though
they fhould never take effect, will ftill afford a pleafing
exercife

exercife to the mind, and contribute to preferve that heavenly difpofition in its full vigour, and make us more ready to purfue and embrace all fuch opportunities as may afterwards be found.

Thus every virtue may, in fome fort, be exercifed, even when all the apparent means of exercifing them are taken away; for our thoughts may ftill be employed in confidering in what manner we would wifh to act, in various circumftances and fituations; and by fuch means as thefe, we may improve ourfelves in every thing that is good and valuable, and enjoy, in fome degree, the good effects of actions which it may never be in our power to perform.

While the thoughts acquire an habit of viewing things in their true light, the pleafures of goodnefs are felt, and the conduct it would dictate is impreffed on the heart, and may remain ready to be called forth to action on future occafions, in fpite of the oppofition which prefent objects and paffions may then make to it.

What improvement as well as fatisfaction may it afford us, to form to ourfelves the moft exalted reprefentation of every virtue—free from every human frailty and imperfection, and raifed far beyond what we have found in real life;—to contemplate them in

R 3   their

their greateſt excellence;—to feel our minds elevated, and our hearts warmed by the repreſentation, while our moſt earneſt deſires are excited to attain to that perfection which we admire; and every difficulty which can oppoſe our efforts, and every ſuffering which may attend them, appear trifling on the compariſon, and unworthy of the attention of an immortal mind. Then to conſider the great and glorious purpoſes for which that mind was intended; the joys which alone can ſatisfy it; the extent of its powers; and the eternity of its duration!

In ſuch contemplations as theſe, the ſoul ſeems to expand itſelf, and enjoy its native excellence; it feels itſelf raiſed above the little objects of this world, and ſeems to make ſome approach to that happineſs for which it was formed, and which even in the midſt of of all that preſent enjoyments can beſtow, and in ſpite of a thouſand diſappointments, it muſt for ever purſue; while the powers and the hopes it feels, afford an earneſt of joys which are calculated to ſatisfy them— for ſurely they were not given in vain.

CHRISTIAN PERFECTION.

———

THERE is no precept in the Gospel of our blessed Saviour delivered more positively than this, " BE YE PERFECT." It is addressed to all, no exception is made in favour of any, and GOD does not require from us what we are unable to perform; yet when we consider the various talents bestowed upon mankind, and the different situations in which we are placed in this world, it seems scarce possible that all should attain to an equal degree of excellence. The powers and faculties of many are confined, the influence of most men extends but to a very small circle; and while they admire at a distance the virtues of those who have moved in a more exalted sphere, and by their actions or sufferings have benefited mankind, and done honour to the religion they profess, they are apt to imagine that as these are heights of excellence to which they never can attain, those precepts which seem to require such exalted

alted perfection cannot relate to them; that to aim at it would be attempting an impoſſibility; and that ſuch endeavours muſt be left to thoſe whoſe powers are greater, and whoſe influence is more extenſive. Yet the precept is general, and therefore certainly cannot relate to any thing that is only in the power of a few.

What then is this Perfection which is thus required of all, and which therefore certainly may be attained by the poor and dependant, the ſick and helpleſs, as well as by the healthy and powerful, the rich and happy?—Perfection, in any created being, muſt mean the higheſt degree of excellence which that being is capable of attaining; abſolute perfection, in the ſtricteſt ſenſe of the word, being an eſſential attribute of GOD alone. It muſt conſiſt in the utmoſt exertion of thoſe powers with which that being has been endued by his Maker, and in applying them all to the beſt purpoſes. But as the powers given to every different order of being, and probably to every individual, are different, the degree of excellence which conſtitutes the perfection of every one muſt alſo be different; and one who has exerted his little talents to the utmoſt, may be much nearer to perfection, than another in appearance greatly ſuperior to him in excellence, but who had talents to have made him much more ſo, if he had employed them as he ought.

This

This muft always occafion great uncertainty in the judgments we form of others, fince we can never know the powers with which they are endued, nor the difficulties with which they are obliged to ftruggle, and therefore can never judge how near they may have advanced to that perfection which it was in their power to attain. Perhaps the fault we think we have difcovered in our neighbour, may have arifen from fome motive unknown to us, which, in the eye of Him who fees the heart, may greatly leffen its malignity. Perhaps, through ignorance or prejudice, it may appear to him in a very different light. Such confiderations fhould make us very cautious in the judgments we pafs upon others, and always inclined to hope the beft, and to give the moft favourable interpretation to every action; fince, for ought we know, it may be the moft juft.

But with regard to ourfelves, the cafe is far different, and we are by no means liable to the fame difficulties; fince the fault we *fee*, we certainly may endeavour to amend; and if that endeavour be fincere, we may be certain that it will be affifted and accepted.

Some good we can all do; and if we do all that is in our power, however little that power may be, we have performed our part, and may be as near perfection as thofe whofe influence extends over kingdoms, and whofe

whofe good actions are felt and applauded by thoufands. But then we muft be fure that we do *all* we
can, and exert to the utmoft all thofe powers which
God has given us; and this is a point in which we
are very apt to deceive ourfelves, and to fhelter our
indolence under the pretence of inability.

Let us then, in whatever fituation in life we may be
placed, confider attentively how we may improve it to
the beft advantage; let us never be difcouraged by any
difficulty which may attend what we know to be our
duty; for if we do our beft, we are fecure of an All-
powerful affiftance; nor let us ever think any occafion
too trifling for the exertion of our beft endeavours, for
it is by conftantly aiming at perfection in every inftance,
that we may at length attain to as great a degree of it
as our prefent ftate will admit of.

Thus we may fulfil our bleffed Saviour's command,
in the meaneft as well as in the moft exalted fituation
in this world; and upon an attentive furvey of every
one, we may difcover duties fufficient to require the
exertion of our utmoft powers, and many opportunities of doing good to ourfelves and others, which are
apt to efcape the eye of a fuperficial obferver. And in
that day when God fhall judge the fecrets of men's
hearts, we fhall probably fee many, who have fcarce
been

been noticed in this world, diftinguifhed amongft the
moft illuftrious followers of their LORD, and preferred
far before others, who while they lived were the general
objects of reverence and admiration.

The poor man, weakened perhaps by ficknefs and
dejected by contempt, whofe daily labours can hardly
procure him a little pitance to fupport his wretched
life, cannot indeed diftinguifh himfelf by any great
actions or public benefits; he cannot feed the hungry,
nor clothe the naked; but he can fubmit with patience
and refignation to that ftate in which Providence has
placed him; he can labour with integrity and diligence
to improve it to the beft advantage, and look up to
GOD for a blefling upon his honeft endeavours; he
can inftruct his children in all the good he knows, and
be always ready to take every opportunity to affift a
neighbour in diftrefs; and in fo doing he may approve
himfelf to the Searcher of Hearts, far more than thofe
who perhaps have inwardly applauded their own benevolence, when they beftowed a trifle out of their fuper-
fluity to give a temporary relief to his diftrefs.   He
may rife to a ftill more heroic degree of excellence, and
lift up a fecret prayer for the man who has refufed
him even that trifle; yet none will hear that prayer,
but HE to whom it is addreffed.   Contempt, or at beft
pity, will be his portion in this life; and probably it
                                                       will

will never occur to any one who fees him, that he shall
hereafter behold him with admiration and reverence—
perhaps with envy.

Let not then the meaneft imagine he can do nothing;
he may be truly great, he may fulfil his Lord's command, and be fecure of his acceptance; but let him
remember, that every advantage muft be gained by
fome effort, and that no fituation can juftify indolence
and inactivity, or murmuring and repining. And let
thofe who fee his diftrefs, but cannot fee his heart,
think in what manner they fhall wifh they had treated
him, if they fhould fee him hereafter approved and rewarded by the great Judge of men and of angels.

But poverty is not the only fituation which is pleaded
as an excufe for the little good that is done; there are
many who live dependant on the will of others, fo that
even their time is not at their own difpofal. When
this is really the cafe, and, from the relation in which
they ftand, fuch a dependance is indeed their duty,
then a cheerful fubmiffion is the virtue which their
fituation particularly requires; and a little experience
will foon convince them that it is not one of thofe
which is moft eafily attained: their own inclinations,
even when juft and reafonable, muft often be facrificed
to the mere whims of another, and it will require no
                                                      fmall

fmall degree of exertion to be able to gain continual victories over themfelves.

Let not thofe who are placed in fuch a fituation imagine, that they can do nothing, for they have much to do; their tafk is difficult and painful; and the more fo, as they muft not expect to be fupported in it by the approbation of others, fince in general the more perfect their virtue, the lefs it will be noticed; they will not tell the world that it cofts them a continual ftruggle, and probably the world will never fufpect it; but on the contrary, they will often be blamed for actions, which, if their true motives were known, would appear moft deferving of applaufe.

Something of this fort may probably have been felt at times by all whofe fituation is in any degree dependant; but that dependance can never be fo continual as to deprive them of all opportunities of acting for themfelves, and benefiting others; and when fuch opportunities are rare, that confideration fhould incite them to exert the utmoft diligence in feeking them out, and activity in making the moft of them.

The fame may be faid in regard to all who complain in any refpect of the narrow fphere in which they are confined. Let them examine it attentively, and conftantly

ftantly and diligently exert their utmoft powers in doing all the good they can, and they will foon find that much more is in their power than they were apt at firft fight to imagine; and this, not only by relieving the diftreffes of poverty and want, by being always ready to give comfort to the afflicted, and advice and inftruction to thofe who ftand in need of them; but common converfation, and daily intercourfe with the world, afford numberlefs opportunities of doing good, to thofe who are attentive to make the moft of them.

A word in feafon may fave the blufh of bafhful merit oppreffed by the torrent of ridicule, or ftop the progrefs of a report, repeated perhaps only from mere thought-lefsnefs, but which yet, when repeated a little farther, might ftain the reputation of real worth.

A gentle anfwer may ftop the violence of paffion in its beginning, which a hafty word, and perhaps even filence, might have aggravated, till the confequences became dreadful indeed.

To relate the diftreffes of thofe who cannot plead for themfelves, may awaken the compaffion of fome who are able to relieve them, and perhaps not unwilling, but too indolent, or too much engaged in other purfuits, to feek out objects for themfelves; nay, fometimes,

times, if the application be made in public, it may gain from vanity what it would not have gained from bene- volence; and by thefe means the poor at leaft will be benefited, and poffibly the rich may be fo too; for thofe who have been induced to do good, though by a wrong motive, may yet find that there is a pleafure in it, and learn in time to love it for its own fake.

A judicious obfervation, a rational maxim, a gene- rous fentiment, when unaffectedly introduced in the courfe of converfation, may make an impreffion on thofe who are not in the habit of thinking for themfelves.

A thoufand little attentions may exercife our own benevolence, and gain the good-will of others; per- haps too they may contribute in fome degree to foothe the aching heart; for even the moft trifling inftance of kindnefs, which fprings from true benevolence, can hardly fail of giving fome pleafure to the receiver.

But it is impoffible to enumerate the opportunities of doing good, which are continually offering them- felves in the daily occurrences of life, in fuch things as are commonly called *little*; though indeed that appella- tion by no means belongs to them, fince it is upon thefe principally that the happinefs of fociety depends; and a want of attention to them is the fource of continual

tinual uneafinefs, and the chief caufe of moft of the unhappinefs which difturbs the intercourfe of private life.

The man of delicate fenfibility, whofe heart has received an unneceffary wound, has been more hurt by
the perfon that gave it, than by him who robbed him
of his purfe; and yet how often is this done without
the leaft remorfe, merely from the idle vanity of difplaying a falfe wit, or a trifling talent for ridicule; or
from a defire of affuming a fuperiority which is feldom
affumed but by thofe who have no title to it.

Opportunities of giving pain are continually prefenting themfelves; and to avoid them is as much a pofitive duty, as to feek opportunities of doing good: both
are alike the genuine effects of true benevolence, which
perhaps fhews itfelf in a ftill ftronger light when it
beftows a relief to the diftreffed; fince, in this laft inftance, the pleafure attending on the action might alone
be a fufficient inducement to it.

But while we are endeavouring to avoid giving pain
to others, we fhould not be lefs cautious to guard
againft a difpofition to take offence at every trifle,
which is not lefs prejudicial to the pleafures and advantages of fociety. A want of delicacy, or perhaps
merely a want of thought, may have given rife to the
expreffion

expreffion which difpleafes us; and if fo, we have no
more right to be offended, than we have when we
fuffer any harm by mere accident; fince, in either of
thefe cafes, there certainly was no intention to hurt us.
Such excufes as thefe we may often find reafon to plead
for others, but we can never plead them in our own cafe,
if we indulge ourfelves in the flighteft word or look
that may give pain to another; fince the firft is what
nobody will own, and a confcioufnefs of the laft would
be a contradiction in terms.   Thus reafon and juftice,
as well as benevolence, and a regard for the good of
fociety, require us to make great allowances for others,
and very little for ourfelves.

It may poffibly be objected, that all this requires an
uncommon degree of reflection and prefence of mind;
that fuch continual watchfulnefs muft reftrain the freedom of converfation; and that it is impoffible to be
always upon our guard.   But fuch objections feem to
fuppofe a continual ftruggle with a bad heart; whereas
he who aims at perfection, muft begin his bufinefs
there; for while any bad difpofitions are encouraged,
it is vain to hope that they will not fometimes fhew
themfelves in words and actions; and it would be a
difficult tafk indeed, always to put on the appearance
of benevolence, while the reality is wanting.   But were
the heart full of love and gratitude to its Creator, and

S   true

true benevolence to its fellow-creatures, it would find in itself the fource of all that is good and pleafing in fociety, and then there would be nothing more to do but to follow its dictates.

To attain to this perfection, and to conquer all thofe felfifh paffions which oppofe it, fhould be our conftant aim, and muft indeed often require the exertion of no fmall effort; but it is an object well worthy to employ our utmoft powers, and it may be obferved for our comfort, that at every ftep the difficulties will leffen; the heart will feel the *pleafure* of benevolence, while reafon and religion recommend the *duty:* every opportunity of exercifing it will increafe this pleafure, and confequently the paffions will become lefs and lefs able to contend with it, till at laft they are obliged to yield, not fo much to reafon as to a ftronger inclination; and then the exercife of benevolence becomes not the refult of reflection, but an indulgence of the bent and inclination of the heart.

To one of this character, it would require no effort to avoid giving pain to others, fince it would be the greateft pain he could himfelf receive. The little vanity of difplaying a fuperiority, or gaining a momentary applaufe, could be no inducement to him, fince the feelings of his own heart would make him blufh while
he

he received it, from a confcioufnefs that he might have deferved applaufe of a much higher kind.

In fhort, to fay that the exercife of this branch of benevolence, which relates to the little occurrences of common converfation, muft lay us under a continual reftraint, is in effect to fay, that fome other inclination is more powerful in the heart; and while that is che-rifhed and encouraged, it is vain to hope that it will not prevail, and perhaps in time quite extinguifh that heavenly fpark, which, properly cultivated, might have been a fource of happinefs to ourfelves and others. To improve this fhould be the conftant bufinefs of every one, in every different fituation in life; for though its exercifes are various, and though in this world they cannot always afford an equal degree of pleafure, yet the principle from which they all flow is ftill the fame; and it is the principle which fhould be cultivated and improved here, and which will be accepted and rewarded hereafter.

There is yet another fituation, which, more than all thofe hitherto mentioned, feems to damp all the powers of the foul, and exclude all means of doing good to ourfelves or others, and that is Sicknefs.

When the body is weakened by pain, the thoughts confufed, and the fpirits funk, we are apt to think it

S 2

is

is no time to aim at perfection, and that we are incapable of making any effort towards it; yet even here we ſhould remember, what has been all along obſerved, that the perfection required of us conſiſts in exerting to the utmoſt thoſe powers which we poſſeſs, however little they may be. In ſuch a ſtate, we cannot indeed act as we would have done in the days of health and ſtrength, but we can ſtill conſtantly and ſincerely endeavour to do our beſt.

In this, as in every other ſituation, we ſhould remember, that to avoid giving pain is as much an act of benevolence as to do real good. An impatient word, or even a groan, may wound the heart of the friend who has been watching night and day to give you eaſe and comfort: ſuppreſs it, and you will have prevented a pang, greater perhaps than that which you relieve when you give bread to the hungry, and drink to the thirſty. An expreſſion of fretfulneſs at the little inadvertencies of attendants may diſcourage well-meant endeavours, while a different conduct might ſtill incite them to do more, and poſſibly in time might teach thoſe, who at firſt were guided merely by intereſt, to act upon a better motive.

Such opportunities of doing good may yet be found; and if ſuch exertions are attended with ſome difficulty, let

let us remember, that to conquer that difficulty is a chief part of the perfection which such a state admits of.

True christian fortitude and patience must be founded on a sincere love of GOD, and an affectionate, filial resignation to his will; and such a disposition must necessarily include benevolence towards all mankind, an *active* principle which pain and sickness never can extinguish.

Let us not then imagine that excess of suffering can be an excuse, if we are conscious that we give any pain to others, which might have been avoided; since it can only be so, for those who are not conscious of it, when it forces from their weakness expressions which they afterwards recollect with pain, and wish they could recall; for it must be allowed, that in such a situation it is difficult to be always upon our guard.

But though this give reason to hope that great allowances will be made, yet it can be no excuse for not exerting our best endeavours; and it is a very powerful motive to induce us to cultivate, whilst we are in health, that heavenly benevolence, which, were it once, as it ought to be, the habitual disposition of the soul, would remain so in every situation in life, and find continual opportunities of exerting itself, even in the midst of pain and sickness, of poverty and affliction.

S 3 It

It would be endlefs to enumerate the variety of fituations in which inability to do good is pleaded as an
excufe for the little that is done, and that not always
by the indolent alone: for there reigns in the world a
certain prejudice in favour of fuch actions as are attended with apparent good effects, which it is very
difficult for any one entirely to fhake off: and it may
have happened to many, whofe intentions were yet
fincerely good, to be difcouraged by the little apparent
good that is in their power, and by the difappointments
they may have met with in their endeavours to do even
that little.

But let fuch remember, that it is the intention, not
the fuccefs, which conftitutes the merit of any action;
and whatever prefent pleafure they may lofe by the
difappointment of their honeft endeavours, will, with
infinite advantage, be made up to them hereafter.

They fhould alfo confider, that the applaufe of man,
and even the fecret felf-approbation which attends a
fuccefsful good action, is not without its danger.
Vanity is ever apt to fteal in, and taint even our beft
performances, and that not only in fuch actions as are
feen by the world, for there may be a vanity even in
our own applaufe: and when they find their beft
endeavours difappointed, and their greateft kindneffes
                                                    received

ceived with indifference and repaid with ingratitude, let them not be difcouraged, but ftill go on in the bleffed courfe in which they are engaged, conftantly endeavouring to difcover and improve every opportunity of doing good, however little it may appear, though no eye fee them, and no voice applaud them.

HE who is higher than the higheft, will mark their diligence, and crown hereafter their fincere endeavours, though he may fee fit to humble them with difappointments here, and deprive them of the fatisfaction of enjoying the good they do.

Indeed fuch difappointments, if rightly ufed, will ferve to improve and fecure their virtues, by exalting them above the influence of all meaner motives, and teaching them to exert their utmoft endeavours, not with a view to any prefent enjoyment, but with a fincere and earneft defire to pleafe Him who will not fail to accept and blefs an unwearied perfeverance in well-doing.

It may alfo be obferved, for their comfort and encouragement, that we are very bad judges of the fuccefs of our endeavours; and if we do not immediately perceive any good effect from them, we have no reafon from thence to conclude that they will have none.

You

You have been endeavouring perhaps to comfort the afflicted, and you have been heard without attention, or even with impatience; yet be not difcouraged: a little reflection may give weight to what you have faid, and a perfeverance in the friendly endeavour may in time make an impreffion upon the heart, and recall it in fome degree to a fenfe of pleafure: for furely no one can be fo entirely overwhelmed with grief, as to receive no pleafure from the expreffions of real kindnefs, or to be quite infenfible to that tender, unwearied attention to give eafe and comfort, which flows from an affectionate and benevolent heart: and when the mind is once awakened from the lethargy of grief, it will by degrees become more compofed, and be capable of liftening to the comforts of Reafon and Religion.

You have, it may be, been giving fome good advice, which in appearance produced no other effect than that of difpleafing the perfon to whom it was addreffed; yet you know not what impreffion it may have made. Our pride is apt to rife at firft againft the very thought of being advifed; yet if the advice were given in fuch a manner as fhewed it to be the effect of real kindnefs and good- will, not of any defire of affuming a fuperiority, it may probably be remembered and examined afterwards. Reafon may approve what pride at firft rejected,

rejected, and the advice may have its weight, though the perfon who gave it may never be informed of his fucccfs.

The fame obfervation might be made in many other inftances; and whoever fincerely endeavours to do all the good he can, will probably do much more than he imagines, or will ever know, till the day when the fecrets of all hearts fhall be made manifeft.

To decline any difficulty which lies in the way of our duty, under pretence of inability to conquer it; to refufe engaging in any good and virtuous undertaking, from a fear that we fhall not fucceed in it; are certainly the effects of cowardice, not of humility.

We know not our powers 'till we exert them; and by exertion we may be very certain they will improve; but indolence is glad of an excufe, and pride fears the mortification of a defeat; and thus every noble and generous effort is difcouraged, and the mind finks into a ftate of inactivity, quite oppofite to that diligent and ardent endeavour after perfection, which fhould be the conftant bufinefs of our lives.

It is by this endeavour that we fulfil the precept of our BLESSED SAVIOUR. We cannot indeed at once

attain

attain to perfection, but the attainment of it may be our conftant aim in the fmalleft as well as in the moft important actions of our lives; and that not only in thofe duties which more immediately belong to our ftation in the world, but in every inftance which may be within our power.

In whatever fituation we may be placed, let us not enquire what allowances may be made for us, nor how much we muft do that we may hope for acceptance. But let us confider what is the *beft* that we can do; for we certainly have not performed our duty, when we are confcious that we might have done better.

Let us endeavour to imprefs upon our hearts fuch a lively fenfe of the kindnefs of our Infinite Benefactor, as may prompt us to embrace every opportunity of ex- preffing our love and gratitude towards Him. We fhall not then be difpofed to confine the circle of our duties; but on the contrary it will be our earneft defire to extend it as far as poffible, that we may enjoy, in every inftance, the delightful thought of acting for *his* fake, and making the beft returns in our power to the infinite obligations we have received.

This will diffufe a fort of heavenly pleafure over the moft trifling circumftances in our lives, fince even in
thefe

thefe we may ftill endeavour to do our beft, from a defire to pleafe Him; and that defire, we may be very certain, will always be accepted.

If this influence our conduct in the daily occurrences of life, every incident that befals us will contribute to bring us nearer to perfection, by furnifhing a frefh opportunity for the exertion of our utmoft endeavours to attain it. Every little difficulty we conquer will increafe our fortitude; every attempt to do good, even in the fmalleft inftance, will ftrengthen our benevolence; even the faults we may fall into, though they humble us under the fenfe of our weaknefs, yet inftead of difcouraging, they will ferve to excite us to redouble our diligence, fince we are certain that, if we will fincerely endeavour to avoid them for the future, we may depend on the Divine Mercy to affift our weaknefs, and pardon our imperfections.

The afflictions we may meet with will be brightened by the thought that they are fent by an All-gracious Father, who would not permit them but for our real advantage; and that therefore they certainly might be fo, if we make a right ufe of them. Inftead of finking under them, we fhall look up to Him with filial confidence; and, rejoicing in his all-powerful protection and affiftance, not only fubmit without murmuring, but

but even be thankful for the trial, and conftantly endeavour fo to receive it, that it may anfwer the gracious purpofes for which it was defigned.

By refigning our own will, upon every little occafion, when it oppofes that of our Maker, we fhall learn to do it in the greateft; and by conftantly aiming at perfection, even in the fmalleft inftances, we fhall make daily advances towards it, till at laft we arrive at that bleffed ftate, where all our imperfections fhall be done away; and perfect goodnefs, and perfect happinefs, fhall reign for ever.

RESIGNATION.

RESIGNATION is a conſtant habitual diſpoſition of mind, by which the true Chriſtian is prepared to give up his own inclination in every inſtance, whether great or ſmall, whenever the will of GOD requires that he ſhould do ſo.

To ſubmit with patience to what we cannot avoid, and reſign with cheerfulneſs what we cannot keep, has been the advice of the wiſe in every age; but without ſome motive to enable us to do ſo, ſuch leſſons generally produce little effect.

To make the beſt of evils for which we can diſcover no remedy, and no conſolation, is a painful effort, which often wears out the ſpirits it pretends to ſupport.

Religion alone can enable us to practiſe that reſignation which it requires, and to practiſe it in every inſtance;

ftance; for we are much too apt to deceive ourfelves by a falfe kind of refignation, which is exerted only on particular occafions, and which in fact is often nothing more than the facrifice of one inclination to another that is more dear to us; and he who has refigned an empire may be as far from that refignation of the *will* which the Chriftian Religion requires, as he who has ufurped one; and he may be as eafily overcome by the little trials which continually arife in common life.

True Refignation muft be founded on a principle which never can be fhaken; it muft be a real fentiment of the heart, infpired by a motive fufficient to excite and to fupport it; and this can be no other than a fincere love of GOD, and that from a confidence which is infpired by the confideration that all events are in the hands of Him whofe wifdom and goodnefs are infinite as his power.

No comfort can fpring from the thought that the evils we fuffer are unavoidable; and the unwilling fub-miffion, which yields to a power it is unable to refift, is far unlike the true refignation of a Chriftian. An apparent calm may, in the one inftance, difguife the fecret murmurs of the heart, or perhaps a painful effort may compel the violence of paffion to give place to the ftillnefs of defpair; but in the other, the ftroke,
                                                              however

however deeply felt, is yet willingly endured; and a firm and affectionate confidence, which no affliction can remove, infpires that fincere refignation, which triumphs over the feelings of nature, though it cannot deftroy them, and always rejoices in the thought that an Almighty Friend will difpofe all events as fhall be moft for the real-intereft of thofe who truly love Him and depend upon Him, however painful their trials may at prefent appear.

The effects of this refignation are not only a peace, which grief itfelf cannot take away, and a conftant readinefs to fubmit to every difpenfation of Providence, but alfo an active and vigorous refolution, which willingly undertakes the moft painful exertions, and performs the tafk affigned, whatever ftruggle it may coft. It is always ready to facrifice whatever is moft dearly valued, when the will of God requires it, and finds a fecret fatisfaction even in the moft painful exertions, from the confideration of Him for whofe fake they are made.

To feel and to enjoy the innocent pleafures which our fituation in this world affords, is not only natural, but laudable. The pleafing as well as the painful circumftances in life are intended for our real advantage; and the fame difpofition of mind, which refigns them

readily

readily when the will of God requires it, will alſo enjoy them while He beſtows them, and enjoy them with
a ſecurity which others can never feel; ſince the
thought of their uncertainty (that conſtant allay to
every earthly pleaſure) is always attended with a full
conviction, that they will be enjoyed as long as is really
beſt for us, and that an All-powerful aſſiſtance will
enable us to ſupport their loſs.

This then is the diſtinguiſhing character of true reſignation :——

It does not conſiſt in giving up any particular thing
which we loved and valued; it is not a virtue which is
only to be called forth to action on extraordinary occaſions ;—but

It is a conſtant and ſettled diſpoſition of mind, ever
ready to conform to the will of God in every inſtance;
to enjoy the pleaſures, or ſubmit to the afflictions which
He ſends, and to *act* or *ſuffer*, as the duties of every
different ſituation may require.

It is the only ſure foundation of patience, fortitude,
ſelf-denial, generoſity, and all thoſe virtues by which a
victory is gained over our own inclinations.   Other
motives may inſpire them in particular inſtances, but
they

they can never be practifed conftantly and univerfally, but by thofe whofe will is fincerely refigned to the will of their Creator.

He who has borne fome confiderable lofs, or great degree of pain, with calm refolution, may grow fretful and uneafy at the little difgufts and mortifications of fociety. He who has gone through the moft difficult trials with that active courage which engages univerfal admiration, may fear to oppofe the current of general practice in trifles, when he thinks he fhall be defpifed for fo doing. And he who has denied himfelf numberlefs indulgencies to affift the diftreffed, may yet find it difficult to give up his particular fancies and inclinations, however neceffary the facrifice may be. But none of thefe things can happen where the heart is fincerely and univerfally refigned.

The moft painful fufferings are patiently endured; the darling inclination is readily and willingly given up, whatever anguifh the facrifice may coft, whenever the Will of God requires it: and when that Will requires facrifices of another kind, the little comforts, conveniences, and amufements of common life; the kindnefs which foothed our afflictions, or the applaufe which fupported our refolution; every thing, in fhort, whatever it may be, which we are called upon to re-

T

fign,

sign, is then the object, in regard to which that virtue is to be exercised; and the heart in which that difpo-fition reigns, is equally prepared for all.

We deceive ourfelves greatly, if we imagine that an extraordinary exertion of refignation in one inftance may difpenfe with it in others which appear to us tri-fling; on the contrary, if ever we find it wanting on thofe little occafions, we have reafon to fufpect that the feeming exertion of it in greater matters was in reality owing to fome other motive.

Much may be refigned by thofe who are far indeed from having refigned their will; and the little trials which pafs unnoticed by all the world, are often the fureft tefts of our fincerity, and may be the moft ufeful to fubdue our perverfe inclinations, and bring us to that ftate of mind which our duty requires.

That the exertions of this virtue are often painful, cannot be denied. Our duty may require us to make great and voluntary facrifices which we might have avoided, or to fubmit to injuries and humiliations which we might have prevented; though even here it is poffible, that the indulgence of our inclinations might in the end have been productive of much greater fufferings, than the denial of them. But in

general

general it is exerted in regard to fuch evils as we cannot prevent; and, according to the obfervation of Dr. Young,

> " That duty gives up little more
> " Than anguifh of the mind."

It is an act of love and confidence which refts in full fecurity on an all-wife and all-powerful *friend*; and confidered in this view, it is a difpofition pleafing in the higheft degree, which foftens all the miferies of life, and converts the moft painful trials into opportunities for exprefling fentiments which are always felt with pleafure,—fuch pleafure as no afflicion can ever take away.

The facrifice was perhaps unavoidable; but whether neceffity or duty required it, to a heart truly refigned, the cafe is juft the fame; in the laft, it will indeed be attended with a peculiar fatisfaction; but in the firft, the manner in which it is received may make it equally a voluntary act. The fame fentiments may be expreffed, and will moft certainly be accepted; the fame comforts may foothe our forrows, and the fame affiftance will fupport us under them. Confidered in this view, refignation is a ftate of mind indifpenfibly neceffary to fecure our happinefs in this world.

It has been the advice of many, that in our happieft days we fhould confider the uncertainty of the good

things

things we poffefs; look forward to the time when we
muft be deprived of them; and prepare ourfelves beforehand to fupport their lofs, by anticipating the pain
we fhall then feel, and rendering the mind in fome
fort familiar to it, that we may be better able to fuftain
the fhock when it comes : thus fecuring to ourfelves a
certain prefent pain, in order to leffen one which is future and uncertain.   Perhaps it may not produce even
this good effect, fince dwelling on the thought of forrows muft certainly by degrees wear out the fpirits, and
render them lefs able to fupport them when they come.

True refignation teaches us another method of preparing ourfelves for afflictions; and while in every
pleafure we feel and enjoy the goodnefs of an indulgent
Father, it refts on Him with full confidence, and is
ready to acquiefce in the moft painful difpenfations
which the fame goodnefs fhall ordain for us;—it does
not anticipate evils, nor allay our pleafures; but it is a
difpofition of mind which enables us to fupport the
one, and enjoy the other.

Afflictions muft come, no efforts can avoid them, or
deftroy the fenfe of them; patience may endure them;
but patience, where the heart is not refigned, is a continual ftruggle with ourfelves.   True refignation alone
furnifhes us with a fure refource; it fubmits with fincere

cere and affectionate confidence, and cafts all our care on Him who careth for us. It is alfo conducive to happinefs, not only by giving peace and fecurity to our pleafures, and comfort to our afflictions; but alfo by leffening the number of thofe afflictions.

An attachment to our own will, is one great fource of the forrows of this life. The heart which is truly refigned, will find no pain or difficulty in many things which to others would be made matter of real forrow; it yields eafily to the prefent ftate of things; complies with the inclinations of others; and gives up its fancies or its pleafures cheerfully and readily, as thefe are never its principal point in view.

Numberlefs little compliances are neceffary in the daily intercourfe of life. To the felfifh, thefe are matter of continual mortification and uneafinefs; for a trifle, which oppofes the will of thofe who are accuftomed to confider their own will in every thing, becomes a matter of importance; but where refignation is become habitual, fuch things make little or no impreffion; they are performed with eafe, and even with pleafure.

In order to the attainment of this difpofition, it is highly neceffary to imprefs ftrongly upon our minds a deep fenfe of the wifdom and goodnefs of the Al-

T 3   mighty;

mighty; of our own blindnefs and inability to judge what is really beft for us, and of the happinefs of being in his hands.

Who can look back on his paft life, without being fenfible, that the difappointment of his wifhes has often been a real advantage to him? A very little attention muft be fufficient to convince us, how apt we are to be milled by our own paffions and prejudices, and how little we know of the confequences of thofe things which are at prefent the objects of our hopes and fears. How often has profperity proved fatal to innocence and virtue, without bringing with it that happinefs which it feemed to promife! And how many have been reduced to the painful conclufion, " that all is vanity!" when perhaps it was too late to begin a new courfe, and choofe " the better part."

Could we look into the hearts of thofe whom the world calls happy, how different fhould we often find the reality from the appearance! In the midft of prof-perity and fuccefs, fome fecret care, the difappointment of fome darling wifh, or even the languor and difguft which fometimes attend fatiety, and deftroy the relifh of pleafure, may be as real evils, and as deftructive of happinefs, as thofe fufferings which are generally the objects of compaffion.

We

We know not what we wifh: and the indulgence of our wifhes would often prove the fource of mifery even in this world; but as to what tends moft to our improvement in what is truly valuable—the ftate which is moft calculated to exercife and improve our virtues, and lead us to eternal happinefs, we are ftill more in the dark.

Not only reafon and obfervation of others, but our own feelings and experience, may convince us of this; and fhew us, even at prefent, that we have great caufe to rejoice that all events are in better hands than ours: though this is a truth which will probably be more fully explained to us hereafter, when we can at one view take in the whole feries of the events of our lives, and know their confequences.

Convinced of this great truth, let us cultivate thofe fentiments which it ought to produce,—that love and confidence which fuch a conviction fhould infpire; and thefe will naturally produce true and fincere refignation.

But as we are not always in a ftate of mind to have recourfe to a train of reafoning; and even the real fentiments of the heart do not always act with the fame force, but may be obfcured for a time by paffion, and the ftrong impreffion of prefent objects; it is of the utmoft confequence to us to endeavour to render every

virtue

virtue familiar and habitual by continual exercife; and there is none for which more frequent opportunities prefent themfelves, than for this of refignation.

Not a day can pafs over us without bringing with it fome things which are not exactly what we could wifh; and all thefe, however trifling, may have their ufe, if we receive them as we ought. All may exercife refignation, and help to keep us in a ftate of mind prepared for greater trials. The bad effects of the contrary are often evident; for often do we fee the good-humour of the morning, and confequently the happinefs of the day, deftroyed by trifles; and if the good effects they might produce, are not as immediately apparent, they are not lefs real, nor lefs important.

The habit of fubmitting to little mortifications, from the beft motives, and of endeavouring to improve by them, will infenfibly connect thofe ideas with every mortification; and the happy effects of this may extend to matters of the greateft confequence, and be felt at a time when the mind is too much affected to feek for comforts which are not familiar to it.

But above all, in order to the attainment of true and conftant refignation, it is highly neceffary to keep up a frequent intercourfe with Heaven, by the exercifes

cifes of devotion. We muft offer up to God our hopes and wifhes, and beg of Him that affiftance which alone can fupport our weaknefs, and which will never be denied to thofe who fincerely feek for it.

It is by true devotion, conftantly felt and exercifed, that true refignation can be fully attained. This furnifhes a refource in every forrow, a fupport in every trial; and where this is truly felt, the heart may indeed be refigned in regard to the events of this world, fince its beft affections, its moft ardent wifhes, are fixed on another.

In the Holy Scriptures we find the neceffity and importance, and alfo the happinefs, of this virtue, fet forth in the ftrongeft terms. Our bleffed Saviour calls us to take up our crofs and follow him,—to be ready to facrifice all that is moft dear to us, even our own life, if we would be worthy of Him.

The Chriftian life is reprefented as a ftate of warfare, in which we muft endure hardfhips as faithful foldiers, and through much tribulation enter into the kingdom of heaven. At the fame time we have the moft comfortable affurances of affiftance and fupport, and the moft engaging invitations to the performance of this duty.

He

He who invites us to take his yoke upon us, at the same time affures us, that in fo doing we fhall find reft to our fouls. We are called to caft our burden upon the Lord; we are affured that He will never leave us nor forfake us; that our prayers fhall be heard, and under the fhadow of his wings we may rejoice. We are promifed affiftance which can never fail, and joy which no man can take from us.

And while we are thus invited to refign ourfelves to the will of GOD, and furnifhed with the moft powerful motives to fupport our refignation, we have at the fame time the moft perfect pattern of that virtue in Him who did no fin, neither was guile found in his mouth; and who yet came not to do his own will, but was obedient unto death, even the death of the crofs.

Such is the leffon that the whole tenor of Scripture inculcates, and fuch the example by which it is enforced!——Happy they on whom thefe confiderations make their due impreffion; whofe hearts are truly refigned, and who are always prepared for the exercife of that virtue on every different occafion!

The exercife of virtue, in many inftances, is attended with fuch pleafures, that even thofe who are not influenced by a fenfe of duty and religion, can hardly be infenfible

infenfible to them; though fuch pleafures are enjoyed in a far higher degree, by thofe in whom thefe fenti- ments prevail. Happy in the thought that their own inclination is then conformed to the will of their Cre- ator, they go " on their way rejoicing" in the good effects of their endeavours; they fee diflrefs relieved, and virtue promoted; they give comfort to the afflict- ed, and advice to the ignorant; and enjoy the innocent pleafures of friendfhip and fociety, by making them ufeful to themfelves and others. Their happinefs is a kind of foretafte of the happinefs of heaven—a happi- nefs which angels might partake, and in which they may indulge their inclination without reftraint, free from any apprehenfion of that fatiety and difguft which often attend the pleafures of this world, or that re- morfe by which they are often fucceeded.

To fuch pleafures we are apt to think we can hardly be too much attached; and yet even thefe we may be called to refign; and to murmur and repine at the lofs of them, may be as much an inflance of the want of true refignation, as the fame would be in any other cafe.

We think our inclinations were innocent, and even laudable; and this feems in fome fort to juftify regret at being no longer able to indulge them; but our in- clinations can be innocent no longer than they are
conform-

conformable to the will of God; any farther attachment to them becomes an attachment to our own will, which it is as much our duty to conquer in this cafe, as in every other.

We delighted to relieve diftrefs; but we are reduced to poverty, and can enjoy that delight no more:—Another tafk is now affigned us, and muft be performed with the fame readinefs.

We poffeffed the power of making thofe happy with whom by duty and affection we were connected, and our lives were fpent in the pleafing and laudable employment:—A change of circumftances has taken that power away; no felfifh regret muft be fo far indulged as to make us neglect the duties which are yet within our power, and become lefs diligent in performing the part allotted to us, becaufe it is lefs pleafing.

We enjoyed the pleafures of friendfhip and fociety, and felt the innocent fatisfaction which attends on the exercife and improvement of the benevolent affections; —but friends may be removed from us; we may be reduced to a ftate of unavoidable folitude, or rendered, by ficknefs or other circumftances, incapable of contributing to the pleafures of converfation and fociety, and reduced to give pain, where we moft wifh to con-
                                                        fer

fer happinefs. Still the fame difpofition muft remain; ftill the regret of pleafure loft, of whatever kind that pleafure might be, will be an inftance of the want of true refignation, whenever it is indulged fo far as to make us in any degree negligent of prefent duties—for that pleafure is the facrifice we are then called to make.

Such facrifices are difficult and painful indeed; and the lofs of innocent and virtuous pleafures muft be ftrongly felt by thofe whofe hearts were difpofed to delight in them. While within their reach, it was their duty to enjoy them; and the lofs of them is attended with the lofs of that felf-fatisfaction, and even of that improvement of good and amiable difpofitions, which was derived from them.

But little do we know, in this frail and imperfect ftate, what tends moft to our improvement; and a fituation which appears to us moft unfavourable to it, may be fuch as is really beft for us. Such indeed we may be fure it is, when Infinite Wifdom and Good- nefs has decreed it for us.

The mind of man is naturally active, and the active duties are always the moft pleafing. Life, deprived of thefe, prefents a blank, more difficult to fupport than even painful exertions which are attended with fuccefs

and

and self-approbation. Virtue is then no longer its own
reward; for silent suffering, when nothing else is in our
power, affords no matter for exultation, but rather
for the contrary, from the thought of the uselessness
of such a life, which necessity itself seems hardly suffi-
cient to justify.

Here then the importance of that true resignation,
which religion inspires, appears in the strongest light,
as well as the happiness attending on it. That life
which once appeared a blank is such no longer, for
our time is still spent in the way most acceptable to
our Creator. Had He required of us " some great
thing," some painful and difficult exertion, it would
certainly have been our duty to have performed it;
perhaps we fancy we could have performed it with
satisfaction; but are we sure that there would have
been no mixture of self-complacence, or even of vanity, in this satisfaction?

Let us try whether we find the same satisfaction in
complying with *his* will in other instances. The necessity of our situation points out to us our duty.

If by sickness, the loss of any of our faculties, or
any other cause, we are really deprived of the power
of employing ourselves in any thing useful, and reduced

duced to a ftate in which a great part of our time muft neceffarily be paffed in doing nothing, it is then evidently the will of GOD that it fhould be fo; and we then conform to *his* will by fubmitting to it as we ought, as we do by performing the active duties when called to them; and we may ftill look up to Him with filial confidence, and enjoy thofe hopes which attend the good and faithful fervant, who conftantly and diligently performs the part affigned him, whatever that part may be.

Every change of circumftances ferves only to vary the tafk we are called to perform, but fhould make no change in the difpofition of the mind, by which alone we are acceptable in the fight of Him who feeth not as man feeth.

Even in the decay of our faculties by age or ficknefs, the fame difpofition muft be ftill preferved. The lively fancy, which amufed our folitary hours, may be loft; the active fpirits, which animated our conduct, and even contributed to the ardour of our devotions, may be impaired; and we may feel (in fpite of all our efforts) that the earthly body preffeth down the mind.

Perhaps there is hardly any inftance in which it is more difficult to preferve a conftant and fincere refignation

nation than in this; yet even in this it may be ftill preferved, and may make our little remaining powers ftill
ufeful to ourfelves, and acceptable to our Creator; ftill
that " peace which paffeth all underftanding," which
nothing in this world can give or take away, may remain in the heart, in the midft of the decay of our
bodily and even of our mental powers; and will do fo,
in a heart which has always been truly refigned to the
will of God in every different ftate.

To bear the infirmities of age with proper fentiments, is a leffon which fhould be learnt in youth;
not by anticipating evils which perhaps we may never
be called to fuffer, but by acquiring and exercifing that
refignation which is neceffary in every ftate, and which,
when rendered conftant and habitual, will remain fo in
every change of circumftances; though it would be
difficult indeed to acquire it in the days of weaknefs
and decline, when the powers of action are in a great
meafure taken away, when every effort is painful, and
when bad habits have been fo long rooted as fcarcely
to be overcome.

O my CREATOR and REDEEMER! whofe goodnefs
to me fhines forth as ftrongly in the afflictions Thou
art pleafed to fend me, as in the bleffings wherewith
thou haft furrounded me; may I enjoy thy bleffings
with

with a cheerful and a grateful heart, yet ever be ready to refign them when it fhall be Thy good pleafure to deprive me of them! And when thou art pleafed to prove me with afflictions, may I always receive them with patience and humility; remembering that they are fent by an indulgent Father, who permits them for my good, and who will affift and fupport me under them!

May I never indulge the leaft repining or difcontented thought; but, fixing my attention on thofe divine joys which Thou haft prepared for them who truly love Thee, may I ever be ready to refign what I moft love and value, when Thou fhalt fee fit to require it of me; and by a conftant endeavour to conform my will to Thine in all the changes of this world, may I at length, through thy infinite mercy, arrive at that heavenly kingdom, where Thou wilt crown our fincere, though imperfect obedience, with everlafting and unchangeable felicity!

F I N I S.

www.ingramcontent.com/pod-product-compliance
Lightning Source LLC
Chambersburg PA
CBHW020505270326
41926CB00008B/751